BECAUSE ...you are AWESOME and a wonder-worker. YOU ARE GOD. JUST YOU.
PSALM 86:10

Celebrate Wonder All Ages is a curriculum that honors the spiritual life of children. *Celebrate Wonder All Ages* will engage children in open-ended exploration and inquiry of the Bible. Through experiential activities, spiritual practices, and reflection, *Celebrate Wonder All Ages* serves as a biblical guide to help children make meaning for their lives. This curriculum seeks to deepen children's faith formation and to create a safe space for children to ask big questions and claim their spiritual identity as children of God.

Please visit **CokesburyKids.com**, where you can find training videos, blog posts, free stuff, and more.

What Is...

Celebrate Wonder All Ages is a curriculum that seeks to celebrate spirituality through wonder. Children are naturally spiritual beings and everyday theologians. We want children to recognize and name this spirituality found within themselves and in all the world around them.

This curriculum is based on spiritual practices, which are incorporated through play, discovery, biblical exploration, faith conversation, and relationship. Children who participate in *Celebrate Wonder All Ages* will come to know and use spiritual practices as a way to deepen their faith and to grow in their spiritual identity as children of God. These spiritual practices then become building blocks for holy moments and enrich the faith lives of each and every child. We hope you will come wonder with us as we celebrate the Spirit of God in the lives of children.

The Components of...

Spiritual Practice

A spiritual practice is an intentional activity or ritual that helps you be aware of God's presence. For children, this means simple and tangible practices to connect to God's love.

Teaching children spiritual practices provides them with tools needed to fully know themselves as children of God. This is important because children who are equipped with these helpful daily practices can develop deeper connections to encounter the divine.

Children are innately spiritual. Their curiosity and wonder are a model for faith in action. Through spiritual practices, they can remain connected to this natural spirituality. Spiritual practices come in all shapes and sizes. In *Celebrate Wonder All Ages,* they are typically simple and interactive practices for the children to develop their own ways to feel God's presence and to know their identity as children of God.

Peaceful Place

The Peaceful Place is a space for the children to spend quiet time with God. Children enjoy having a comfortable place with quiet activities when they are feeling stressed or overwhelmed. Create a feeling of softness and rest by using soft rugs, pillows, and stuffed animals to snuggle with in the area. Each week there will be suggested books and quiet activities you can choose from. Since you know your children and what they need, you are also invited to include your own contributions to the Peaceful Place.

Wonder Table

A Wonder Table is similar to a worship altar found in many worship spaces. It is a holy space meant to help the children see and know God is present. We encourage you to use a smaller table that the children can see and interact with.

Each week there are suggested items to place on the table that coordinate with the church liturgical year and the Bible story. Suggested items include a Bible, a candle, a colored cloth, and so forth. The table can be used as a gathering area for the story time and for participating in spiritual practices.

Wonder Box

The Wonder Box is a place to hold a special item that connects to the Faith Word and to the Bible story. Each week there will be a suggested item to place in the box. The Wonder Box is very special and is kept on the Wonder Table. Each week you will reveal what is inside and discuss its importance.

We encourage you to make your own Wonder Box. It can be any shape or size, but it's best if it has a lid. You can create your own box for the children, or you may wish to include the children in the creation process. The goal is for the children to come to know this box as very special. The Wonder Box is another way for the children to engage in the Bible story and to focus on the lesson.

Core Resources

CELEBRATE WONDER ALL AGES has been adapted to make it easy for ministry with children and families to happen, no matter what your church's current reality is. Whether you're meeting in person all in one room, sending materials home for families to use together, offering a large group opening and small groups in person or virtually, or hosting an intergenerational gathering for your whole church, CELEBRATE WONDER ALL AGES will work for you. The CELEBRATE WONDER ALL AGES Kit contains a Leader Guide, Reproducible Kids' Book, Class Pack, and CD-ROM! The CD-ROM has digital copies of the Leader Guide and Reproducible Kids' Book.

Kit:
Leader Guide
Reproducible Kids' Book
Class Pack
CD-ROM

Core Resources

Celebrate Wonder DVD

The *Celebrate Wonder DVD* features a child host who will engage the children through storytelling, life application, and exploration of the Faith Word. The DVD includes a music video and thirteen sessions (one for each Sunday) that are 3–5 minutes each.

CEB Bible

This interactive Bible includes four-color icons and illustrations throughout, with a wealth of notes, historical facts, book introductions, devotionals, and other interactive elements to capture inquisitive young minds. The *Deep Blue Kids Bible* encourages a thirst for God's timeless message. For children ages 7–12.

Celebrate Wonder Bible Storybook

A colorfully illustrated children's Bible storybook that will engage the children through simple storytelling and open-ended questions that encourage the children to wonder about the Bible story and make connections between the Bible and their lives. Includes 150 stories!

Supplies

These are basic supplies you will want to have readily available.
All supplies will be listed above the activity in the Leader Guide.

Box of tissues

Card stock

CD player

Chenille stems

Colored and white
copy paper

Colored pencils

Computer and
printer

Construction paper

Cotton balls

Cotton swabs

Crayons

DVD player

Glue, gluesticks

Handwashing
supplies

Index cards

Lunch-sized paper
bags

Markers (washable
and permanent)

Metal brads

Mural paper

Napkins

Paintbrushes

Paper bowls

Paper clips

Paper cups

Paper or plastic table
coverings

Paper plates

Paper punch

Paper streamers

Paper towels

Pencils

Plastic containers for
paint and water

Posterboard

Projector or
television

Resealable plastic
bags

Ribbon

Scissors (adult and
safety)

Smocks

Stapler, staples

Stickers

Tape (clear, masking,
and double-stick)

Tissue paper

Washable paint

Watercolor paints

Watercolor pencils

Wet wipes

Wooden craft sticks

Yarn

But the fruit of the Spirit is love, joy, peace, patience, kindness, goodness, faithfulness, gentleness, and self-control. (Galatians 5:22)

Pentecost – Acts 2:1-41

Prepare to Wonder

Faith Word: SPIRIT

As Christians we celebrate Pentecost as the "birthday of the church." Pentecost originated as a Jewish festival. Pentecost was one of three pilgrimage feasts when Jews gathered in Jerusalem. Jesus had told the disciples to wait in Jerusalem for the gift of the Holy Spirit. It was a time of uncertainty for Jesus' followers. It is likely they were anxious and scared. During this time of waiting in Jerusalem, the disciples and other followers of Jesus were celebrating Pentecost. While they were celebrating, the Spirit arrived. The Spirit arrived sounding like a violent wind and appearing like small flames of fire. Jesus promised to send the disciples a helper and now it had arrived.

The excitement surrounding the arrival of the Holy Spirit attracted a crowd. Not everyone in the crowd was immediately convinced of the Spirit's presence. Some joked they were witnessing the effects of strong wine. Spirit-filled Peter responds to this accusation and begins to preach. About three thousand believers were baptized that day.

The Spirit did not just come to the disciples, but to each person gathered there. The Spirit empowered God's people and gave them courage to continue to spread the good news about Jesus. We may not hear rushing wind or see flames of fire descending on one another, but God's Spirit continues to empower us and give us the courage to do God's work.

The concept of the Holy Spirit is sometimes a difficult one for children and adults to understand. It is okay to admit to your children that you don't have all the answers. Mystery is a part of faith.

Spiritual Practice for Adults

Find a quiet place to sit. Place your feet on the ground and place your palms down on your knees. Take a deep breath in and let it go. This time as you breathe in, think, "Spirit, guide me." Exhale and think, "All my days." Repeat several times.

Come Together

Come Together

Supplies: Class Pack, Celebrate Wonder Bible Storybook, *Wonder Box, red cloth, battery-operated candle, dove*

Prepare Ahead: Set up a Wonder Table (see p. 3) with a red cloth, battery-operated candle, and a Wonder Box (see p. 3). Display the Unit 1 Bible Verse Poster (Class Pack—pp. 10 & 15) and Faith Word Poster (Class Pack—p. 22). Place the dove inside the Wonder Box.

- Point to the Unit 1 Faith Word Poster (Class Pack—p. 22), and invite the children to wonder about what the word *Spirit* means.

- Invite the kids to join you in a circle.

SAY: This month we are going to hear stories about the Holy Spirit and the ways it guides the followers of Jesus.

- In this curriculum, we recommend reading stories from the *Celebrate Wonder Bible Storybook.* Allow an elementary-age child to read the story, "Pentecost" (pp. 268–89) from the storybook.

PRAY: Dear God, thank you for the Holy Spirit. Amen.

Pentecost – Preschool

Supplies: Reproducible Kids' Book, crayons

Prepare Ahead: Photocopy "Pentecost" (Reproducible 1A) for each child.

- Invite the preschoolers to use crayons to color the picture.

SAY: The followers of Jesus waited for the special gift of the Holy Spirit.

WONDER: What is it like to wait for a special gift?

Hidden Letters – Younger Elementary

Supplies: Reproducible Kids' Book, crayons

Prepare: Photocopy "Hidden Letters" (Reproducible 1B) for each child.

- Hand out a copy of "Hidden Letters" to each child.

SAY: Jesus told his disciples to wait for a special gift. One day, a big gust of wind filled the room they were in and small flames appeared. The gift of the Holy Spirit had arrived!

- Invite the kids to look for and circle the letters to the word Spirit.

Holy Spirit Acrostic – Older Elementary

Supplies: Reproducible Kids' Book, pencils or markers

Prepare Ahead: Photocopy "Holy Spirit Acrostic" (Reproducible 1C) for each child.

• Hand out a copy of "Holy Spirit Acrostic" to each child.

SAY: Jesus told his disciples to wait for a special gift. One day, a big gust of wind filled the room they were in and small flames appeared. The gift of the Holy Spirit had arrived!

• Invite the kids to wonder about what words or phrases about God begin with the letters in the words, *Holy Spirit.*

• Encourage them to write these words or phrases next to the appropriate letter.

Dove Banner – All Ages

Supplies: Reproducible Kids' Book, mural paper, crayons, scissors, markers, gluesticks

Prepare Ahead: Photocopy "Dove" (Reproducible 1D) onto card stock for each kid in your class. Cut a long piece of mural paper. Use a marker to write the word "Pentecost" in bubble letters in the center of the paper.

• Show the children the mural paper.

SAY: Today is Pentecost, and we are celebrating the gift of the Holy Spirit.

• Encourage each child to use crayons or markers to cover the mural paper with red, yellow, and orange designs and the dove paper with designs in shades of blue.

SAY: When the disciples received the gift of the Holy Spirit, they saw flames above each other's heads and heard the sound of a rushing wind.

• Invite each child cut out the doves and glue them to the banner.

• Invite the children to color in the letters on the banner.

• Hang the banner up in your room.

Wonder Time

Interactive Bible Story

Supplies: *Reproducible Kids' Book*

Prepare Ahead: *Photocopy "Pentecost" (Reproducible 1F) for each child.*

• Invite several readers to take turns reading the story.

WONDER: Why do you think the Holy Spirit came with licks of fire and wind? What else could the Holy Spirit come with?

Share a Story

Supplies: *Celebrate Wonder DVD, TV, DVD player*

• Invite the children to join you and to sit in a circle on the floor.

• Watch the Session 1 video (Celebrate Wonder DVD).

Wonder with Me

Supplies: *Class Pack, Wonder Box, scissors*

Prepare Ahead: *Lay out the Wonder Story Mat for Unit 1 (Class Pack—pp. 11 & 14). Cut out the Bible story figures (Class Pack—p. 6).*

• Place the Wonder Box on the Unit 1 Wonder Story Mat.

• Show the children the Unit 1 Faith Word Poster (Class Pack—p. 22).

SAY: Today's faith word is *Spirit*. The word *Spirit* means the feeling that God is with you.

• Show the children this week's figure—the symbols of Pentecost.

WONDER together:

  ○ What is your favorite part of this week's story?

  ○ What does it feel like when God is with you?

  ○ What symbol would you make for this week's story?

• Place the figure on the Wonder Story Mat.

• Open the Wonder Box to reveal the dove.

WONDER: Why do you think a dove is in the Wonder Box this week?

Experience Wonder

Wind Painting

Supplies: paper, paint (blue and white), art smocks, paper or plastic table covering, straws

Prepare Ahead: If your paint is thick, use water to thin it so that it will be easier to blow across the paper. Cover the table with paper or plastic.

- Have the children wear smocks to protect clothing.

SAY: Today we will hear the story of Jesus' disciples receiving the gift of the Holy Spirit. The Spirit arrived amid the sound of wind and the appearance of flames.

ASK: What is wind? (*moving air*)

SAY: Today you will use your air to paint a picture.

- Give each child a piece of paper and a straw.

SAY: I am going to put some paint on your paper. Use the straw I have given you to blow the paint around on the paper to make it look like fire.

- Put some blue paint on each child's paper.
- Encourage the children to use the straws to gently blow the paint around on the paper.
- Add a bit of white paint to each child's paper.
- Encourage children to keep blowing the paint around on the paper.
- Set the paintings aside to dry.

Examine the Bible Verse

SAY: Our Unit 1 Bible verse is Galatians 5:22. Find it in your Bibles.

ASK: Is Galatians in the Old or New Testament? (*New*) Where is the Letter to the Galatians located in the New Testament? (*ninth book*) In what chapter of Galatians is our verse located? (*5*) What is the verse number? (*22*)

SAY: Our Bible verse tells us what a life of faith following the Spirit looks like.

- Gather the kids around the Bible Verse Poster (Class Pack—pp. 10 & 15). Read it together.

Peaceful Place

Supplies: Leader Guide—p. 113, Celebrate Wonder Bible Storybook, book: The Day When God Made Church: A Child's First Book About Pentecost, by Rebekah McLeod Hutto; paper; crayons or markers

Prepare Ahead: Photocopy the Unit 1 Faith Word coloring sheet (Leader Guide—p. 113) for each child.

- Assist the children, as needed, as they interact with the items provided.

- Invite the children to make birthday cards that will be given away to the other children on their birthdays.

- Have each child color the Faith Word coloring sheet.

Tip: All of the supplies/activities suggested for the Peaceful Place are optional.

Go in Peace

Spiritual Practice – Exploring the Spirit Through Guidance

SAY: A spiritual practice is something we do to help us be present with God. A spiritual practice can be anything because you can be with God any time, anywhere, and any way! This month we are going to do a guided prayer to connect with God.

- Guide the children through a spiritual practice:

  ○ Find a quiet place to sit. Place your feet on the ground and place your hands palms down on your knees. Take a deep breath in and let it go. This time as you breathe in, think, "Spirit, guide me." Exhale and think, "My whole life." Repeat several times.

SAY: The Spirit will be with each of us for our whole lives. The Spirit will keep us connected to God and each other.

PRAY: Repeat after me: "God, thank you for the Holy Spirit. Help me to feel how close you always are to me. Amen."

- Bless the children before they leave. Touch each child as you say this blessing: "May you feel God's love all around you every day."

Family Spiritual Practice

Supplies: Reproducible Kids' Book; Leader Guide—pp. 111, 112

Prepare Ahead: Photocopy "Celebration Chart" (p. 111) and "Family Letter" (p. 112) for each child.

SAY: Let's take a look at your Take-Home Pages (*Reproducibles 1F–1G*). Ask your family to read the Bible story and participate in this week's spiritual devotion with you. There's an extra activity for you to do sometime this week.

- Send home a copy of the Take-Home Pages, a copy of the Family Letter, and a copy of the Celebration Chart with each child.

Supplemental Activities

Preschoolers – Pentecost Headbands

Supplies: Reproducible Kids' Book; red, orange, and yellow markers; tape; scissors

Prepare Ahead: Photocopy "Pentecost Headbands" for each child. Cut the pieces apart for each child

SAY: Today is Pentecost and we are going to make Pentecost headbands to celebrate. When the Holy Spirit came to the disciples, it appeared as if they had flames on their heads. We will use flame colors—red, yellow, and orange—to make our headbands.

- Invite each child to color and decorate the pieces of their Pentecost Headbands.

- Help each child put together their headbands using tape.

- Encourage the children to wear their headbands.

Early Elementary – Chalk Art

Supplies: dark-colored construction paper (black, brown, or dark blue), chalk (red, orange, yellow, blue, and white), paper towels, newspapers or plastic table coverings

Prepare Ahead: Cover the work area with newspapers or plastic table coverings.

- Have each child choose a dark-colored piece of construction paper.

SAY: Today we are celebrating Pentecost. On Pentecost, the Holy Spirit arrived appearing like flames and sounding like rushing wind.

- Encourage each child to use red, orange, and yellow chalk to draw flames on his or her paper.

- Encourage each child to use blue and white chalk to draw gusts of wind on her or his paper.

- Show the children how to use a paper towel to blend colors of chalk together.

- Let the children experiment with blending the chalk colors together.

Older Elementary – Wind Surfer

Supplies: paper, scissors, tape

- Give each pair of children a piece of paper.
- Have each pair of children fold the paper in half bringing the long edges together.
- Encourage the children to fold the paper in half in the same direction again.
- Have each pair of children cut their paper along the fold lines.
- Let each child take two of the resulting paper strips.
- Encourage each child to stack his or her two pieces of paper on top of one another so the edges are even.
- Have each child lay the two pieces of paper on a table with the long edges at the top and bottom.
- Have each child slide the top piece of paper approximately one and one-fourth inches to the left and use a small piece of tape to secure the two pieces at the short edge of the top strip.
- Have each child turn his or her pieces of paper over and use a small piece of tape to secure the two pieces on the other side.
- Have each child hold the wind surfer in the center of one of the strips of paper and toss it upwards into the air. The wind surfer should open up and spin as it floats to the ground.

ASK: What is separating the two parts of the wind surfer and making it spin? (*wind, air currents*) How do you know that is what's happening? Can you see the wind? (*No, but you can see the effect of the wind.*)

SAY: Today we are celebrating Pentecost. On the first Pentecost when the Holy Spirit descended on the disciples and other followers of Jesus, there was a sound like the rush of a mighty wind. The Holy Spirit, like the wind, is something we cannot see.

Intergenerational Activity – Church Birthday Party

Supplies: party hats, cupcakes, party decorations

Tip: Plan a birthday party for the church.

SAY: Pentecost is the birthday of the church. We're going to celebrate!

- Invite the participants to have fun celebrating the church's birthday.

But the fruit of the Spirit is love, joy, peace, patience, kindness, goodness, faithfulness, gentleness, and self-control. (Galatians 5:22)

Philip and the Ethiopian – Acts 8:26-40

Prepare to Wonder

Faith Word: SPIRIT

Today's Bible story is about the Holy Spirit at work in the life of Philip. The story of the interaction between Philip and the Ethiopian is an example of the amazing things that happen when followers of Jesus allow the Spirit to guide their actions and words.

The Ethiopian was an important official who was responsible for the treasury of the Ethiopian queen. In spite of his status, Jews at that time would have considered him an outsider for two reasons: because of where he lived and because he was a eunuch. In spite of this, the Ethiopian man was seeking God. He had been to Jerusalem to worship and was on his way home when the Spirit sent Philip his way.

Philip, one of Jesus' disciples, had been preaching in Samaria when the Spirit told him to take the road leading from Jerusalem to Gaza. On that road Philip encountered the chariot carrying the Ethiopian man. The Spirit guided Philip to keep up with the chariot. As Philip ran by the chariot, he heard the Ethiopian reading aloud as was customary at the time. Philip recognized that the man was reading from the scroll of Isaiah. Philip asked the man if he understood what he was reading and the man invited him to explain it. At this invitation Philip told the Ethiopian the good news about Jesus. To one who was considered an outcast, hearing about Jesus who welcomed society's outcasts must have been amazing. The Ethiopian man ended up asking Philip to baptize him before the Spirit led Philip elsewhere.

Spiritual Practice for Adults

Find a quiet place to sit. Place your feet on the ground and place your hands palms down on your knees. Take a deep breath in and let it go. This time as you breathe in, think, "Spirit, guide me." Exhale and think, "All my days." Repeat several times.

Come Together

Come Together

Supplies: *Class Pack, Celebrate Wonder Bible Storybook, Wonder Box, green cloth, battery-operated candle, scroll*

Prepare Ahead: *Set up a Wonder Table (see p. 3) with a green cloth, battery-operated candle, and a Wonder Box (see p. 3). Display the Unit 1 Bible Verse Poster (Class Pack—pp. 10 & 15) and Faith Word Poster (Class Pack—p. 22). Place the scroll inside the Wonder Box.*

- Point to the Unit 1 Faith Word Poster (Class Pack—p. 22), and invite the children to wonder about what the word *Spirit* means.

- Invite the kids to join you in a circle.

SAY: This month we are going to hear stories about the Holy Spirit and the ways it guides the followers of Jesus. This week we will hear about a man named Philip.

- In this curriculum, we recommend reading stories from the *Celebrate Wonder Bible Storybook*. Allow an elementary-age child to read the story, "Philip and the Ethiopian" (pp. 276–77) from the storybook.

PRAY: Dear God, thank you for the Holy Spirit. Amen.

Philip and the Ethiopian – Preschool

Supplies: *Reproducible Kids' Book, crayons*

Prepare Ahead: *Photocopy "Philip and the Ethiopian" (Reproducible 2A) for each child.*

- Invite the preschoolers to use crayons to color the picture.

SAY: Philip was lead by the Spirit to a road heading to a place called Gaza. While he was on the road, he met a man from Ethiopia.

WONDER: Why do you think the Spirit led Philip to go to where the Ethiopian was?

What Doesn't Belong? – Younger Elementary

Supplies: *Reproducible Kids' Book, crayons*

Prepare: *Photocopy "What Doesn't Belong?" (Reproducible 2B) for each child.*

- Hand out a copy of "What Doesn't Belong?" to each child.

SAY: Philip was lead by the Spirit to a road and he met a man from Ethiopia. The man was reading Scripture, but he wasn't sure what it meant. Philip helped the man understand that it was about Jesus.

- Invite the kids to look for and circle what doesn't belong in the picture.
- Encourage the kids to color the picture.

What Does It Say? – Older Elementary

Supplies: Reproducible Kids' Book, pencils or markers

Prepare Ahead: Photocopy "What Does It Say?" (Reproducible 2C) for each child.

- Hand out a copy of "What Does It Say?" to each older elementary child.

SAY: The Holy Spirit led one of Jesus' followers named Philip to an Ethiopian man who was reading Scripture. The Ethiopian man didn't understand what he was reading, so Philip helped him. The sentence below is a jumbled version of Acts 8:35. Can you unscramble each word so that the Scripture verse makes sense?

- Invite the kids to unscramble the Bible verse.
- Encourage them to use a Bible if they get stuck.

Thank-You Cards – All Ages

Supplies: Reproducible Kids' Book, card stock, crayons or markers

Prepare Ahead: Photocopy "Thank-You Cards" (Reproducible 2D) onto card stock for each kid in your class.

SAY: The Ethiopian man was thankful to Philip for teaching him about Jesus. Who are you thankful for? Make a thank-you card for that person.

- Encourage each child to use crayons or markers to color and decorate their cards.
- Invite them to fold the card in half and write a message on the inside of the card.
- Encourage the kids to give or mail the card to the person they are each thankful for.

Wonder Time

Interactive Bible Story

Supplies: Reproducible Kids' Book

Prepare Ahead: Photocopy "Philip and the Ethiopian" (Reproducible 2F) for each child.

- Invite several readers to take turns reading the story one section at a time.

WONDER: What is your favorite part of this story? Why?

Share a Story

Supplies: Celebrate Wonder DVD, Celebrate Wonder Bible Storybook, TV, DVD player

• Invite the children to join you and to sit in a circle on the floor.

• Watch the Session 2 video (Celebrate Wonder DVD).

Wonder with Me

Supplies: Class Pack, Wonder Box, scissors

Prepare Ahead: Lay out the Wonder Story Mat for Unit 1 (Class Pack—pp. 11 & 14). Cut out the Bible story figures (Class Pack—p. 6) if you haven't already.

• Place the Wonder Box on the Unit 1 Wonder Story Mat.

• Show the children the Unit 1 Faith Word Poster (Class Pack—p. 22).

SAY: Today's faith word is *Spirit*. The word *Spirit* means the feeling that God is with you.

• Show the children this week's figure—one of the symbols of baptism.

WONDER together:

    ○ What is the most important part of the story?

    ○ What does it feel like when God is with you?

    ○ What symbol would you make for this week's story?

• Place the figure on the Wonder Story Mat.

• Open the Wonder Box to reveal the scroll.

WONDER: Why do you think a scroll is in the Wonder Box this week?

Experience Wonder ————————

Interconnected Web

Supplies: ball of yarn

• Invite the kids to sit in a circle.

SAY: Today we heard the story of Philip and the Ethiopian. These two people didn't know each other before the story, but by the end of it, they were connected.

ASK: What does it mean to be connected to another person?

SAY: I think it means that we are a part of each other's story. I think it means what I do affects other people. I think it means that I am called to show God's love to other people. It's like all of us are a web.

- Show the kids the ball of yarn.

SAY: I am going to hold onto the end of the yarn ball and toss the yarn across the circle. The person who catches it will hold onto the yarn and then toss the yarn ball to another person. By the end of the game, we will have a web.

- Hold onto the end of the yarn ball and toss the yarn across the circle.

- The person who catches the yarn will hold onto the yarn and toss the yarn ball to another person. The yarn will unwind as it goes, forming visual connections between the kids.

- Keep tossing the yarn ball across the circle making a web. It's okay if kids get to catch and toss the yarn ball more than once.

WONDER: How is this web like people?

Examine the Bible Verse

SAY: Our Unit 1 Bible verse is Galatians 5:22. Find it in your Bibles.

ASK: Is Galatians in the Old or New Testament? *(New)* Where is the Letter to the Galatians located in the New Testament? *(ninth book)* In what chapter of Galatians is our verse located? *(5)* What is the verse number? *(22)*

SAY: Our Bible verse tells us what a life of faith following the Spirit looks like.

- Gather the kids around the Bible Verse Poster (Class Pack—pp. 10 & 15). Read it together.

Peaceful Place

Supplies: Leader Guide—p. 113, Celebrate Wonder Bible Storybook, book: Welcome Child of God, by Anne Ylvisaker; paper; crayons or markers

Prepare Ahead: Photocopy the Unit 1 Faith Word coloring sheet (Leader Guide—p. 113) for each child.

- Assist the children, as needed, as they interact with the items provided.

- Invite the children to draw a picture of their favorite part of today's story.

- Have each child color the Faith Word coloring sheet.

Tip: All of the supplies/activities suggested for the Peaceful Place are optional.

Go in Peace

Spiritual Practice – Exploring the Spirit Through Guidance

SAY: A spiritual practice is something we do to help us be present with God. A spiritual practice can be anything because you can be with God any time, anywhere, and any way! This month we are going to do a guided prayer to connect with God.

- Guide the children through a spiritual practice:
  - ○ Find a quiet place to sit. Place your feet on the ground and place your hands palms down on your knees. Take a deep breath in and let it go. This time as you breathe in, think, "Spirit, guide me." Exhale and think, "My whole life." Repeat several times.

SAY: The Spirit will be with each of us for our whole lives. The Spirit will keep us connected to God and each other.

PRAY: Repeat after me: "God, thank you for the Holy Spirit. Help me to feel how close you always are to me. Amen."

- Bless the children before they leave. Touch each child as you say this blessing: "May you feel God's love all around you every day."

Family Spiritual Practice

Supplies: Reproducible Kids' Book; Leader Guide—pp. 111, 112

Prepare Ahead: Photocopy "Celebration Chart" (p. 111) and "Family Letter" (p. 112) for each child.

SAY: Let's take a look at your Take-Home Pages (*Reproducibles 2F–2G*). Ask your family to read the Bible story and participate in this week's spiritual devotion with you. There's an extra activity for you to do sometime this week.

- Send home a copy of the Take-Home Pages, a copy of the Family Letter, and a copy of the Celebration Chart with each child.

Supplemental Activities

Preschoolers – Pretend to Be the Sunday School Teacher

Supplies: none

SAY: Philip taught the Ethiopian man about God and Jesus.

ASK: Who teaches you about God and Jesus?

SAY: I'd love to see you each teach each other about God and Jesus. Can you pretend to be a Sunday school teacher?

- Invite each child pretend to teach today's Bible story, or another story about God and Jesus.

Early Elementary – Follow the Spirit

Supplies: none

SAY: Today Philip followed the nudge of the Holy Spirit and made a new friend! Let's play a game to remember to follow the Spirit.

- Play a variation of the game, "Follow the Leader."
- Invite the kids to follow you and mirror your actions.
- After a few minutes, invite a child to become the leader. The rest of the group will follow that child and mirror their actions.
- After a few minutes, invite another child to become the leader. Keep playing until each child has gotten to be the leader.

Older Elementary – Ethiopian Cross

Supplies: Reproducible Kids' Book, world map or globe, cardboard, pencils or pens, scissors, aluminum foil, craft sticks, double-stick tape, transparent tape

Prepare Ahead: Photocopy "Ethiopian Cross" (Reproducible 2E) for each child.

SAY: Our Bible story today is about one of Jesus' followers, named Philip, and a man from Ethiopia.

- Have the children find Ethiopia on the map.

SAY: Today you are going to make an Ethiopian cross.

- Give each child a copy of "Ethiopian Cross."

SAY: This cross looks a little different than the crosses we are used to seeing. Each arm of the cross is the same length and there are three points on the end of each arm to represent the Trinity.

ASK: Do you remember what the Trinity is? *(the idea of God as Father, Son, and Holy Spirit)*

SAY: Ethiopian crosses are often silver-plated and decorated with elaborate designs.

- Encourage each child to cut out the cross pattern and use it to draw a cross on a piece of cardboard.
- Have each child cut out a cardboard cross.

- Give each child a piece of aluminum foil slightly larger than the cardboard cross.

- Encourage each child to place a piece of double-stick tape on one side of the cardboard cross and then turn the cross over and press it firmly to the non-shiny side of the foil.

- Have each child use a pair of scissors to snip from the edge of the foil almost to the cardboard at each corner and point of the cross.

- Encourage each child to carefully wrap the foil around the cross, smoothing the edges, overlapping the foil on the back, and folding the foil back so loose edges are not visible from the front.

- Have each child use transparent tape to tape the foil down on the back of the cross.

- Invite each child to use a craft stick or a non-opened ballpoint pen to press designs carefully into the foil on the front of the cross.

Intergenerational Activity – Isaiah 53:1-2

Supplies: Bibles, paper, pencils

SAY: Philip helped an Ethiopian man understand the words he was reading. The Ethiopian man was reading from the scroll of Isaiah. Isaiah is in the Old Testament. At the time Philip met the Ethiopian man the New Testament hadn't been written yet.

- Have the participants to look up Isaiah 53:1-2 in their Bibles.

- Invite a participant to read the verses aloud.

ASK: If somebody asked you what these verses mean, what would you tell them?

- Give each participant a piece of paper and a pencil. Encourage each participant to rewrite Isaiah 53:1-2 in their own words.

- Invite participants to share their writings with the group.

SAY: The Spirit guided Philip letting him know where to go and what to do next.

ASK: How do you figure out what God wants you to do?

PRAY: God, thank you for loving us and claiming us as your own. Help us to pay attention to the things you are asking us to do so that we might share your love with others. Amen

But the fruit of the Spirit is love, joy, peace, patience, kindness, goodness, faithfulness, gentleness, and self-control. (Galatians 5:22)

Spiritual Gifts – 1 Corinthians 12:1-11

Prepare to Wonder

Faith Word: SPIRIT

Today's Bible story is from one of the letters Paul wrote to the church at Corinth.

During his missionary travels, Paul helped establish the church at Corinth and became friends with the followers there. After helping the church get established, Paul left the community to start another.

While Paul was continuing his missionary journey, he heard that the Christians in Corinth were struggling and arguing among themselves. Some scholars think he may have gotten a letter from the Corinthians. However Paul found out, the community was quarreling over who was most important.

Paul wrote to his friends at Corinth to remind them that each person is important in his or her own way. Paul's letter outlines that every gift, skill, and talent come from the same Spirit rendering a hierarchy pointless. Each gift—wisdom, knowledge, faith, healing, miracles, prophecy, languages—are all gifts of the spirit.

Spiritual Practice for Adults

Find a quiet place to sit. Place your feet on the ground and place your hands palms down on your knees. Take a deep breath in and let it go. This time as you breathe in, think, "Spirit, guide me." Exhale and think, "All my days." Repeat several times.

Come Together

Come Together

Supplies: *Class Pack,* Celebrate Wonder Bible Storybook, *Wonder Box, green cloth, battery-operated candle, mirror*

Prepare Ahead: *Set up a Wonder Table (see p. 3) with a green cloth, battery-operated candle, and a Wonder Box (see p. 3). Display the Unit 1 Bible Verse Poster (Class Pack—pp. 10 & 15) and Faith Word Poster (Class Pack—p. 22). Place the mirror inside the Wonder Box.*

- Point to the Unit 1 Faith Word Poster (Class Pack—p. 22), and invite the children to wonder about what the word *Spirit* means.

- Invite the kids to join you in a circle.

SAY: This month we are going to hear stories about the Holy Spirit and the ways it guides the followers of Jesus. This week we will read a letter Paul wrote to believers in a town called Corinth.

- In this curriculum, we recommend reading stories from the *Celebrate Wonder Bible Storybook.* Allow an elementary-age child to read the story, "Spiritual Gifts" (pp. 300–301) from the storybook.

PRAY: Dear God, thank you for the Holy Spirit. Amen.

Spiritual Gifts – Preschool

Supplies: *Reproducible Kids' Book, crayons*

Prepare Ahead: *Photocopy "Spiritual Gifts" (Reproducible 3A) for each child.*

- Invite the preschoolers to use crayons to color the picture.

SAY: Paul wrote a letter to people to remind them that everyone has special gifts. Each gift can be used to make the world better together.

WONDER: What is your special gift?

What Makes Me, Me? – Younger Elementary

Supplies: Reproducible Kids' Book, crayons

Prepare: Photocopy "What Makes Me, Me?" (Reproducible 3B) for each child.

• Hand out a copy of "What Makes Me, Me??" to each child.

SAY: Paul wrote a letter to people to remind them that everyone has special gifts. Each gift can be used to make the world better together.

SAY: One way to know what your special gifts are is to learn more about yourself.

ASK: What makes you special and unique?

• Invite the kids to fill in the reproducible worksheet.

• Encourage the kids to share their worksheets with the class so they can learn more about each other too.

Self-Portrait – Older Elementary

Supplies: Reproducible Kids' Book, colored pencils or markers

Prepare Ahead: Photocopy "Self-Portrait" (Reproducible 3C) for each child.

• Hand out a copy of "Self-Portrait" to each child.

SAY: Paul wrote a letter to people to remind them that everyone has special gifts. Each gift can be used to make the world better together.

SAY: You are special! Draw a self-portrait that shows how special you are.

• Invite each kid to draw a self-portrait.

• Encourage the kids to share their portraits with the class so they can learn more about each other too.

Memory Verse Puzzle – All Ages

Supplies: Reproducible Kids' Book, card stock, crayons or markers, scissors

Prepare Ahead: Photocopy "Memory Verse" (Reproducible 3D) onto card stock for each kid in your class.

SAY: Paul wrote lots of letters. Our memory verse is from the letter Paul wrote to the followers of Jesus who lived in the town Galatia.

• Give each child a copy of the puzzle.

• Invite one of the kids to read the memory verse to the class.

• Encourage each child to use crayons or markers to color and decorate their puzzles.

• Invite them to cut out their puzzles. You may need to help the youngest kids.

• Encourage the kids to put their puzzles together and read the verse.

Wonder Time

Interactive Bible Story

Supplies: Reproducible Kids' Book

Prepare Ahead: Photocopy "Spiritual Gifts" (Reproducible 3F) for each child.

• Invite several readers to take turns reading the story one section at a time.

WONDER: What other gifts, skills, and talents does the Spirit give?

Share a Story

Supplies: Celebrate Wonder DVD, TV, DVD player

• Invite the children to join you and to sit in a circle on the floor.

• Watch the Session 3 video (Celebrate Wonder DVD).

Wonder with Me

Supplies: Class Pack, Wonder Box, scissors

Prepare Ahead: Lay out the Wonder Story Mat for Unit 1 (Class Pack—pp. 11 & 14). Cut out the Bible story figures (Class Pack—p. 6) if you haven't already.

• Place the Wonder Box on the Unit 1 Wonder Story Mat.

• Show the children the Unit 1 Faith Word Poster (Class Pack—p. 22).

SAY: Today's faith word is *Spirit*. The word *Spirit* means the feeling that God is with you.

• Show the children this week's figure—a symbol of collaboration (working together).

WONDER together:

  ❍ When have you worked together with someone?

  ❍ What does is feel like when God is with you?

  ❍ What symbol would you make for this week's story?

• Place the figure on the Wonder Story Mat.

• Open the Wonder Box to reveal the mirror.

WONDER: Why do you think a mirror is in the Wonder Box this week?

Experience Wonder

Collaborative Tower Building

Supplies: index cards, tape

• Divide the kids into teams of four.

SAY: Paul encouraged the followers of Jesus to celebrate the gifts, skills, and talents everyone brings to the group. Paul wanted them to work together instead of competing.

SAY: You're going to work together to build a tower.

• Give each team a deck of index cards.

• Encourage the teams to build a tower using the index cards and tape. They can be as creative as they'd like!

WONDER: Why would God want us to work together?

Examine the Bible Verse

SAY: Our Unit 1 Bible verse is Galatians 5:22. Find it in your Bibles.

ASK: Is Galatians in the Old or New Testament? *(New)* Where is the Letter to the Galatians located in the New Testament? *(ninth book)* In what chapter of Galatians is our verse located? *(5)* What is the verse number? *(22)*

SAY: Our Bible verse tells us what a life of faith following the Spirit looks like.

• Gather the kids around the Bible Verse Poster (Class Pack—pp. 10 & 15). Read it together.

Peaceful Place

Supplies: Leader Guide—p. 113, Celebrate Wonder Bible Storybook, book: We All Sing with the Same Voice, by J. Philip Miller & Sheppard M. Greene; paper; crayons or markers

Prepare Ahead: Photocopy the Unit 1 Faith Word coloring sheet (Leader Guide—p. 113) for each child.

• Assist the children, as needed, as they interact with the items provided.

• Have each child color the Faith Word coloring sheet.

Tip: All of the supplies/activities suggested for the Peaceful Place are optional.

Go in Peace

Spiritual Practice – Exploring the Spirit Through Guidance

SAY: A spiritual practice is something we do to help us be present with God. A spiritual practice can be anything because you can be with God any time, anywhere, and any way! This month we are going to do a guided prayer to connect with God.

- Guide the children through a spiritual practice:
  - ○ Find a quiet place to sit. Place your feet on the ground and place your hands palms down on your knees. Take a deep breath in and let it go. This time as you breathe in, think, "Spirit, guide me." Exhale and think, "My whole life." Repeat several times.

SAY: The Spirit will be with each of us for our whole lives. The Spirit will keep us connected to God and each other.

PRAY: Repeat after me: "God, thank you for the Holy Spirit. Help me to feel how close you always are to me. Amen."

- Bless the children before they leave. Touch each child as you say this blessing: "May you feel God's love all around you every day."

Family Spiritual Practice

Supplies: Reproducible Kids' Book; Leader Guide—pp. 111, 112

Prepare Ahead: Photocopy "Celebration Chart" (p. 111) and "Family Letter" (p. 112) for each child.

SAY: Let's take a look at your Take-Home Pages *(Reproducibles 3F–3G)*. Ask your family to read the Bible story and participate in this week's spiritual devotion with you. There's an extra activity for you to do sometime this week.

- Send home a copy of the Take-Home Pages, a copy of the Family Letter, and a copy of the Celebration Chart with each child.

Supplemental Activities

Preschoolers – Collaborative Art

Supplies: butcher paper, crayons or markers

SAY: Paul wanted the people to work well together.

ASK: When have you worked together with a friend or brother or sister?

SAY: Let's work together on an art project!

• Invite the kids to draw a banner of hearts.

Early Elementary – Unity Wreath

Supplies: construction paper, scissors, pencils, paper plate, glue

SAY: Paul wanted the people to work well together.

ASK: When have you worked together with a friend or brother or sister?

SAY: Let's work together on an art project!

• Have each child choose a piece of construction paper.

• Invite them to trace a hand onto their construction paper.

• Help them cut their handprints out.

• Encourage the kids to make a wreath out of their handprints by gluing them to a paper plate.

• Hang the unity wreath somewhere in your space.

Older Elementary – Alike and Different

Supplies: none

SAY: Paul encouraged the followers of Jesus to celebrate the gifts, skills, and talents everyone brings to the group. Paul wanted them to work together instead of competing.

ASK: How can you contribute to our community?

SAY: Part of working together includes learning about each other. Let's learn more!

• Have the children line up on one side of the room.

• Invite the children run to the center of the room when you say something they have or do.

- Say the following things:
  - ○ Run to the center of the room if you have a sibling.
  - ○ Run to the center of the room if you play sports.
  - ○ Run to the center of the room if you like to read books.
  - ○ Run to the center of the room if you have a cat.
  - ○ Run to the center of the room if you have a dog.
  - ○ Run to the center of the room if you like to make art.
  - ○ Run to the center of the room if you have to do chores.
  - ○ Run to the center of the room if you have a favorite color.
  - ○ Run to the center of the room if you play an instrument.
  - ○ Run to the center of the room if you like to travel.
- You are welcome to make up other things like this list too.

Tip: If your space is small, encourage children to walk quickly instead of running.

Intergenerational Activity – Support a Church Project Together

Prepare Ahead: Work with your church staff to decide on a project that your group can work on together.

SAY: Paul encouraged the followers of Jesus to celebrate the gifts, skills, and talents everyone brings to the group. He wanted the followers in Corinth to respect each other and to work together.

ASK: What are some ways our church members work together?

SAY: We're going to work together on a project at our church.

- Invite the participants to do a project together.

But the fruit of the Spirit is love, joy, peace, patience, kindness, goodness, faithfulness, gentleness, and self-control. (Galatians 5:22)

Fruit of the Spirit – Galatians 5:22-23

Prepare to Wonder

Faith Word: SPIRIT

Today's Bible story is from one of the letters Paul wrote to the church at Galatia.

During his missionary travels, Paul helped establish the church at Galatia and became friends with the followers there. After helping the church get established, Paul left the community to start another.

While Paul was continuing his missionary journey, he heard that there were other Christian missionaries teaching the people that all Gentiles had to practice Jewish customs, primarily the custom of circumcision. Paul wrote to the believers in Galatia to tell them this wasn't true and to discourage them from listening to the missionaries encouraging them to do so.

Part of the letter to the Galatians encourages the believers to turn away from things that keep them from living a spiritual life. If they live a spiritual life the fruit of the spirit would grow in their lives. The "fruit of the Spirit is love, joy, peace, patience, kindness, generosity, faithfulness, gentleness, and self-control." These feelings, actions, and values are still important goals for us now.

Spiritual Practice for Adults

Find a quiet place to sit. Place your feet on the ground and place your hands palms down on your knees. Take a deep breath in and let it go. This time as you breathe in, think, "Spirit, guide me." Exhale and think, "All my days." Repeat several times.

Come Together

Come Together

Supplies: Class Pack, Celebrate Wonder Bible Storybook, Wonder Box, green cloth, battery-operated candle, heart

Prepare Ahead: Set up a Wonder Table (see p. 3) with a green cloth, battery-operated candle, and a Wonder Box (see p. 3). Display the Unit 1 Bible Verse Poster (Class Pack—pp. 10 & 15) and Faith Word Poster (Class Pack—p. 22). Place the heart inside the Wonder Box.

- Point to the Unit 1 Faith Word Poster (Class Pack—p. 22), and invite the children to wonder about what the word *Spirit* means.

- Invite the kids to join you in a circle.

SAY: This month we have been hearing stories about the Holy Spirit and the ways it guides the followers of Jesus. This week we will read a letter Paul wrote to believers in a town called Galatia.

- In this curriculum, we recommend reading stories from the *Celebrate Wonder Bible Storybook*. Allow an elementary-age child to read the story, "Fruit of the Spirit" (pp. 306–307) from the storybook.

PRAY: Dear God, thank you for the Holy Spirit. Amen.

Fruit of the Spirit – Preschool

Supplies: Reproducible Kids' Book, crayons

Prepare Ahead: Photocopy "Fruit of the Spirit" (Reproducible 4A) for each child.

- Invite the preschoolers to use crayons to color the picture.

SAY: The Spirit is in each of us. One way we know the Spirit is in us is by the way we behave. When we show love, or are patient, we are showing that the Spirit is in us.

Can You Spot the Hearts? – Younger Elementary

Supplies: Reproducible Kids' Book, crayons

Prepare: Photocopy "Can You Spot the Hearts?" (Reproducible 4B) for each child.

- Hand out a copy of "Can You Spot the Hearts?" to each child.

SAY: The Spirit is in each of us. One way we know the Spirit is in us is by the way we behave. When we show love, or are patient, we are showing that the Spirit is in us.

- Invite the kids to find and circle the hearts in the picture.

- Encourage the kids to color the pictures.

Word Search – Older Elementary

Supplies: *Reproducible Kids' Book, pencils or pens*

Prepare Ahead: *Photocopy "Word Search" (Reproducible 4C) for each child.*

- Hand out a copy of "Word Search" to each child.

SAY: This month, we heard stories about the Spirit. Find and circle words from this month's stories.

- Encourage the kids to find and circle the words from this month's sessions.

June Stars and Constellations – All Ages

Supplies: *Reproducible Kids' Book*

Prepare Ahead: *Photocopy "June Stars and Constellations" (Reproducible 4D) for each child.*

- Hand out copies of Reproducible 4D.
- Invite the kids to look over the stars, constellations, and star pictures on the page.

ASK: Do you recognize any of the star pictures on the page?

- Invite the kids to share any star pictures they recognize. This sheet shows the same stars and constellations that we saw in May. Use this opportunity to see if any kids in your class have tried to find star pictures in the sky.

SAY: This fall, we began looking at the night sky to see star pictures. If you are having trouble finding these shapes, here's a tip.

- Point to Orion on the star chart.

SAY: Orion is the figure of a man. His belt has three bright stars that are pretty easy to find in the winter sky. If you can find the belt, you might be able to find some of the other stars and constellations on the sheet.

- Invite the kids to take the sheets home and look at the sky.

Wonder Time

Interactive Bible Story

Supplies: Reproducible Kids' Book

Prepare Ahead: Photocopy "Fruit of the Spirit" (Reproducible 4F) for each child.

• Invite several readers to take turns reading the story one section at a time.

WONDER: What other feelings or actions are of the spirit?

Share a Story

Supplies: Celebrate Wonder DVD, TV, DVD player

• Invite the children to join you and to sit in a circle on the floor.

• Watch the Session 4 video (Celebrate Wonder DVD).

Wonder with Me

Supplies: Class Pack, Wonder Box, scissors

Prepare Ahead: Lay out the Wonder Story Mat for Unit 1 (Class Pack—pp. 11 & 14). Cut out the Bible story figures (Class Pack—p. 6) if you haven't already.

• Place the Wonder Box on the Unit 1 Wonder Story Mat.

• Show the children the Unit 1 Faith Word Poster (Class Pack—p. 22).

SAY: Today's faith word is *Spirit*. The word *Spirit* means the feeling that God is with you.

• Show the children this week's figure—a symbol for prayer and living spiritually.

WONDER together:

　　○ What fruit of the spirit is hard for you?

　　○ What fruit of the spirit is easy for you?

　　○ What does is feel like when God is with you?

　　○ Why do you think Paul chose these feelings and actions instead of others?

• Place the figure on the Wonder Story Mat.

• Open the Wonder Box to reveal the heart.

WONDER: Why do you think a heart is in the Wonder Box this week?

Experience Wonder

Watercolor Painting

Supplies: card stock, watercolor paints, paintbrushes, cups of water

SAY: Paul wrote a letter to the believers in Galatia to encourage them to live well and to follow the Spirit. When we follow the spirit, we are loving, joyful, peaceful, patient, kind, good, faithful, gentle, and have self-control.

ASK: How would you illustrate living following the Spirit?

- Give each kid a piece of card stock and paints.

- Encourage the kids to paint a picture of what living a life following the spirit could look like.

- If a child needs an idea, they could paint a picture of showing love or kindness to another person.

- Invite the kids to show the group their paintings.

Examine the Bible Verse

SAY: Our Unit 1 Bible verse is Galatians 5:22. Find it in your Bibles.

ASK: Is Galatians in the Old or New Testament? *(New)* Where is the Letter to the Galatians located in the New Testament? *(ninth book)* In what chapter of Galatians is our verse located? *(5)* What is the verse number? *(22)*

SAY: Our Bible verse tells us what a life of faith following the Spirit looks like.

- Gather the kids around the Bible Verse Poster (Class Pack—pp. 10 & 15). Read it together.

Peaceful Place

Supplies: Leader Guide—p. 113, Celebrate Wonder Bible Storybook, book: Maybe God is Like That Too, *by Jennifer Grant; fruit seeds; magnifying glass; paper; crayons or markers*

Prepare Ahead: Photocopy the Unit 1 Faith Word coloring sheet (Leader Guide—p. 113) for each child.

- Assist the children, as needed, as they interact with the items provided.

- Invite the children to explore fruit seeds.

- Have each child color the Faith Word coloring sheet.

Tip: All of the supplies/activities suggested for the Peaceful Place are optional.

Go in Peace

Spiritual Practice – Exploring the Spirit Through Guidance

SAY: A spiritual practice is something we do to help us be present with God. A spiritual practice can be anything because you can be with God any time, anywhere, and any way! This month we are going to do a guided prayer to connect with God.

- Guide the children through a spiritual practice:
  - ○ Find a quiet place to sit. Place your feet on the ground and place your hands palms down on your knees. Take a deep breath in and let it go. This time as you breathe in, think, "Spirit, guide me." Exhale and think, "My whole life." Repeat several times.

SAY: The Spirit will be with each of us for our whole lives. The Spirit will keep us connected to God and each other.

PRAY: Repeat after me: "God, thank you for the Holy Spirit. Help me to feel how close you always are to me. Amen."

- Bless the children before they leave. Touch each child as you say this blessing: "May you feel God's love all around you every day."

Family Spiritual Practice

Supplies: Reproducible Kids' Book; Leader Guide—pp. 111, 112

Prepare Ahead: Photocopy "Celebration Chart" (p. 111) and "Family Letter" (p. 112) for each child.

SAY: Let's take a look at your Take-Home Pages (*Reproducibles 4F–4G*). Ask your family to read the Bible story and participate in this week's spiritual devotion with you. There's an extra activity for you to do sometime this week.

- Send home a copy of the Take-Home Pages, a copy of the Family Letter, and a copy of the Celebration Chart with each child.

Supplemental Activities

Preschoolers – Growing Flowers From Seed

Supplies: potting soil, clear plastic cups, plastic spoons, flower seeds, water

SAY: The Spirit helps us grow in wisdom, love, and truth. Water, sunshine, and soil help flower seeds grow into pretty flowers. Let's grow some flowers that help us remember that we are growing in the spirit.

- Give each child a cup. Help them fill the cup 3/4 of the way with soil.
- Give each child a spoonful of seeds and a spoon.
- Encourage them to bury the seeds in the soil.
- Invite the kids to get a spoonful of water to water their seeds.
- Send the starter plants home with the children.

Early Elementary – Share the Joy

Supplies: Reproducible Kids' Book, card stock, markers or crayons, scissors

Prepare Ahead: Photocopy "Share the Joy" (Reproducible 4E) onto card stock for each child.

SAY: One of the fruit of the Spirit is joy. Joy is a deep happiness that we feel no matter what is happening in our lives. It's a happy, hopeful feeling. Let's share joy with others.

- Give each child a copy of "Share the Joy."
- Encourage them to color the cards.
- Help them cut out the six cards.
- Invite them to give the six cards to six people who need cheering up this week.

Older Elementary – Adding Fruit

Supplies: paper, pens or pencils

SAY: Paul wrote a letter to the believers in Galatia to encourage them to live well and to follow the Spirit. When we follow the Spirit, we are loving, joyful, peaceful, patient, kind, good, faithful, gentle, and have self-control.

ASK: What other attributes might we be if we were to follow Jesus' teachings? *(No answer is incorrect. Some suggestions are empathetic, honest, and active in our community.)*

SAY: These are great ideas! Let's add another verse to our memory verse that includes these attributes.

- Invite the kids to write their new verses onto paper with pens and pencils.

- Encourage them to share their verses with the class.

Intergenerational Activity – Fruit of the Spirit Charades

Supplies: nine index cards, marker

Prepare Ahead: Write a fruit of the Spirit on each index card: love, joy, peace, patience, kindness, goodness, faithfulness, gentleness, and self-control

SAY: Paul wrote a letter to the believers in Galatia to encourage them to live well and to follow the Spirit. When we follow the Spirit, we are loving, joyful, peaceful, patient, kind, good, faithful, gentle, and have self-control.

SAY: We're going to take turns acting out the fruit of the Spirit and seeing if we can guess which one is being acted out.

- Invite a participant to draw a card.

- Encourage that participant to act out the card.

- Invite the other participants to guess what the card attribute is.

- Continue playing until everyone has gotten to act out a card.

Let every living thing praise the LORD! Praise the LORD! (Psalm 150:6)

David Dances – 2 Samuel 6:12-19

Prepare to Wonder

Faith Word: PRAISE

Upon first reading, the sixth chapter of 2 Samuel appears to be a joyous celebration of God, with dancing and instruments and food! This is true, but there is more significance to this Scripture passage then simply an encouragement to celebrate God with dancing.

The chapter centers around the movement of the sacred chest of God–the chest that is called by the name of the Lord of heavenly forces, who sits enthroned on the winged creatures. Sometimes referred to as the ark of the covenant, the chest contained the stone tablets given to Moses on Mt. Sinai. The Israelites viewed the chest as a symbol of God's presence. The chest had not been lost, but it had been neglected. Not any more–the chest was now being transported to Jerusalem.

King David was personally involved with the movement of the sacred chest. He did not simply order some of his men to transport the chest, which he presumably could have, but rather was present and a part of the procession as the chest was moved. It could be said, and it was probably true, that David participated in the ceremony because of an intense, personal connection and relationship to God.

But it was also true that the movement of the chest to Jerusalem was a smart and savvy political move on David's part. Bringing the chest to Jerusalem served to identify the city as a religious center in addition to being the royal capital. This brought the political and religious centers together in one place. Doing so publicly proclaimed that David ruled in alliance with God. Even considering all that, there is joyful dancing, instrument playing and eating! God is worthy of celebration! Enjoy celebrating God with your children this week.

Spiritual Practice for Adults

Find some time to praise God through dancing! Put on your favorite song and cut loose.

Come Together

Come Together

Supplies: Class Pack, Celebrate Wonder Bible Storybook, Wonder Box, green cloth, battery-operated candle, dancer

Prepare Ahead: Set up a Wonder Table (see p. 3) with a green cloth, battery-operated candle, and a Wonder Box (see p. 3). Display the Unit 2 Bible Verse Poster (Class Pack—pp. 12 & 13) and Faith Word Poster (Class Pack—p. 4). Place the dancer inside the Wonder Box.

- Point to the Unit 2 Faith Word Poster (Class Pack—p. 4), and invite the children to wonder about what the word *praise* means.

- Invite the kids to join you in a circle.

SAY: This month we will hear stories about praising God. This week we will hear about King David and how he praised God through dancing.

- In this curriculum, we recommend reading stories from the *Celebrate Wonder Bible Storybook*. Allow an elementary-age child to read the story, "David Dances" (pp. 96–97) from the storybook.

PRAY: Dear God, we are so grateful for you and all of our blessings. Amen.

David Dances – Preschool

Supplies: Reproducible Kids' Book, crayons

Prepare Ahead: Photocopy "David Dances" (Reproducible 5A) for each child.

- Invite the preschoolers to use crayons to color the picture.

SAY: King David praised God by dancing!

ASK: How do you praise God?

Match the Dancers – Younger Elementary

Supplies: Reproducible Kids' Book, crayons

Prepare: Photocopy "Match the Dancers" (Reproducible 5B) for each child.

- Hand out a copy of "Match the Dancers" to each child.

SAY: King David led the parade of musicians and Jewish priests. While King David led the parade, he danced in praise. There are lots of ways to dance in praise.

- Invite the kids to draw a line to match the dancers.

Ark of the Covenant – Older Elementary

Supplies: Reproducible Kids' Book, markers or crayons

Prepare Ahead: Photocopy "Ark of the Covenant" (Reproducible 5C) for each child.

• Hand out a copy of "Ark of the Covenant" to each child.

SAY: King David danced while he led the parade of musicians and Jewish priests who were carrying the ark of the covenant.

• Invite three kids to each read a section of the page to the class.

• Encourage the kids to color the picture of the ark of the covenant.

Dance – All Ages

Supplies: Reproducible Kids' Book, crayons or markers

Prepare Ahead: Photocopy "Dance" (Reproducible 5D) for each child.

• Hand out copies of "Dance" (Reproducible 5D) to each child.

SAY: King David led the parade of musicians and Jewish priests. While King David led the parade, he danced in praise. There are lots of ways to dance in praise. Let's try a few ways!

• Invite the kids to mirror you as you lead them through the four dance moves.

ASK: What is your favorite dance move?

• Invite the kids who would like to share a favorite dance move to show the class.

SAY: King David praised God through dancing.

ASK: What is your favorite way to praise God?

Wonder Time

Interactive Bible Story

Supplies: Reproducible Kids' Book

Prepare Ahead: Photocopy "David Dances" (Reproducible 5F) for each child.

• Invite several readers to take turns reading the story one section at a time.

WONDER: Why do you think David chose to dance instead of playing an instrument with the other people in the parade?

Share a Story

Supplies: Celebrate Wonder DVD, TV, DVD player

• Invite the children to join you and to sit in a circle on the floor.

• Watch the Session 5 video (Celebrate Wonder DVD).

Wonder with Me

Supplies: Class Pack, Wonder Box, scissors

Prepare Ahead: Lay out the Wonder Story Mat for Unit 2 (Class Pack—pp. 8 & 17).
Cut out the Bible story figures (Class Pack—p.19).

• Place the Wonder Box on the Unit 2 Wonder Story Mat.

• Show the children the Unit 2 Faith Word Poster (Class Pack—p. 4).

SAY: Today's faith word is *praise*. Praise is one of the many ways we thank God.

• Show the children this week's figure—a ballet dancer.

WONDER together:

○ How do you think the people felt when they saw the king dancing?

○ What are you thankful for?

○ What is your favorite way to praise God?

• Place the figure on the Wonder Story Mat.

• Open the Wonder Box to reveal the dancer.

WONDER: Why do you think a dancer is in the Wonder Box this week?

Experience Wonder

Dancing Musical Chairs

Supplies: one chair for each child, kids' music, a way to play the music

• Prepare Ahead: Make a circle using the chairs.

SAY: King David danced in the big parade! What dance moves do you think he did?

• Invite the kids to do dance moves like King David.

SAY: We're going to play musical chairs, but instead of walking around our circle of chairs, we will dance around our circle!

• Turn on the music and invite the kids to dance around the circle of chairs.

• After about ten seconds, stop the music and encourage the kids to sit in a chair.

- Remove one chair and begin again.

- Continue to play until one person is left.

- As you play, encourage the kids who aren't in play anymore to dance during the music.

- Play until everyone is ready to move on.

Examine the Bible Verse

SAY: Our Unit 2 Bible verse is Psalm 150:6. Find it in your Bibles.

ASK: Is Psalms in the Old or New Testament? *(Old)* Where is the Book of Psalms located in the Old Testament? *(nineteenth book, almost exactly in the center of the Bible)* In what chapter of Psalms is our verse located? *(150)* What is the verse number? *(6)*

SAY: Our Bible verse is all about praising God!

ASK: What's your favorite way to praise God?

- Gather the kids around the Bible Verse Poster (Class Pack—pp. 12 & 13). Read it together.

Peaceful Place

Supplies: Leader Guide—p. 114, Celebrate Wonder Bible Storybook, *book:* The Last Stop on Market Street, *by Matt de la Pena; music; paper; crayons or markers*

Prepare Ahead: Photocopy the Unit 2 Faith Word coloring sheet (Leader Guide—p. 114) for each child.

- Assist the children, as needed, as they interact with the items provided.

- Invite the children to explore music and dancing.

- Have each child color the Faith Word coloring sheet.

Tip: All of the supplies/activities suggested for the Peaceful Place are optional.

Go in Peace

Spiritual Practice – Exploring Praise Through Worship

SAY: A spiritual practice is something we do to help us be present with God. A spiritual practice can be anything because you can be with God any time, anywhere, and any way! This month we are going to praise God through gratitude.

- Guide the children through a spiritual practice:

  ❍ **SAY:** We're going to think about five things we're grateful for. You'll close your eyes and I will say a place. You will think of something you are thankful for at that place.

  ❍ **SAY:** Get comfortable and close your eyes.

  ❍ **SAY:** At home, I am grateful for…

  ❍ **SAY:** At school, I am grateful for…

  ❍ **SAY:** In nature, I am grateful for…

  ❍ **SAY:** At church, I am grateful for…

  ❍ **SAY:** At the park, I am grateful for…

SAY: We can praise God for all of the things we are grateful for.

ASK: Would any of you like to share what you are grateful for?

PRAY: Repeat after me: "God, thank you for our many blessings. Help us always be ready to praise you. Amen."

- Bless the children before they leave. Touch each child on the hand as you say this blessing: "May you feel God's love all around you every day."

Family Spiritual Practice

Supplies: Reproducible Kids' Book; Leader Guide—pp. 111, 112

Prepare Ahead: Photocopy "Celebration Chart" (p. 111) and "Family Letter" (p. 112) for each child.

SAY: Let's take a look at your Take-Home Pages *(Reproducibles 5F–5G)*. Ask your family to read the Bible story and participate in this week's spiritual devotion with you. There's an extra activity for you to do sometime this week.

- Send home a copy of the Take-Home Pages, a copy of the Family Letter, and a copy of the Celebration Chart with each child.

Supplemental Activities

Preschoolers – Freeze Dance

Supplies: music, a way to play the music

SAY: King David led the parade of musicians and Jewish priests. While King David led the parade, he danced in praise. There are lots of ways to dance in praise.

SAY: Let's dance in praise too! When the music is on, do your best praise dances. When the music stops, you must freeze in your best dancer pose!

• Turn on the music and invite the kids to dance in praise.

• Turn off the music and invite the kids to freeze in their best dancer poses.

• Continue playing until the group is ready to move on.

Early Elementary – Dancing Follow the Leader

Supplies: music, a way to play the music

SAY: King David led the parade of musicians and Jewish priests. While King David led the parade, he danced in praise. There are lots of ways to dance in praise.

SAY: We're going to take turns leading the group like David led the parade. Whoever is the leader will do a dance move and we will do it too!

• Turn on some music.

• Do a dance move and invite the kids to mirror it.

• Choose a child to lead the dancing next.

• After a few minutes, choose another child to lead the dancing.

• Continue in this way until everyone has had an opportunity to lead the dancing.

Older Elementary – Act It Out

Supplies: *Reproducible Kids' Book*

Prepare Ahead: *Photocopy "Act It Out" (Reproducible 5E) for each child.*

SAY: We're going to act out today's story for the younger kids.

- Give each child a copy of the script (Reproducible 5E).
- Invite the kids to choose parts.
- Encourage them to practice the skit a couple of times through until they feel comfortable.
- Perform the skit for the younger groups.

Intergenerational Activity – Ark of the Covenant Craft

Supplies: *Reproducible Kids' Book*

Prepare Ahead: *Photocopy "Ark of the Covenant" (Reproducible 5C) for each participant.*

SAY: King David danced while he led the parade of musicians and Jewish priests who were carrying the ark of the covenant. The ark of the covenant represented God's presence with the Jewish people. King David wanted to bring it to the city of Jerusalem where he lived.

ASK: What sorts of things remind us of God's presence with us today?

SAY: We're going to break into groups of four and make our own ark of the covenants out of building bricks. Bonus points for building one of the things that remind you of God's presence today too!

- Divide the participants into groups of four.
- Invite the participants to build the ark of the covenant out of building bricks.
- Encourage groups to show their creations to the whole group.

Let every living thing praise the LORD! Praise the LORD! (Psalm 150:6)

Shout With Joy – Psalm 100

Prepare to Wonder

Faith Word: PRAISE

Sometimes we equate joy with happiness and it is true that the two emotions are similar. However, if God is deserving of our joyful praise, surely that is not true only when we are happy. Even in the midst of sadness or confusion, it is possible for joy to exist as the assurance that God is with us in the midst of whatever we are experiencing or feeling. God is our God and is faithful no matter what. Now there's a reason to be joyful.

Psalms is often referred to as the prayer book or the hymnbook of the Bible. The Psalms have played a significant part in the worship life of God's people for many years. Many of the psalms were written for use in corporate worship, while others are the prayers of individuals. Psalms continues to play a significant role in both Jewish and Christian worship as well as being used for individual prayer and devotion.

In Psalms we find a reflection of the entire range of human emotion. There are psalms expressing sadness, joy, anger, happiness, despair, hope, fear, and trust. This aspect of Psalms provides a couple of valuable reassurances. First of all, whatever you are feeling, you are not alone in that experience; one of the psalmists has felt your pain or experienced your doubt or celebrated your joy. Secondly, you may take any emotion or situation to God in prayer. It is a good and appropriate thing to offer our entire human experience to God. The structure of Psalm 100 is typical of a song of praise. It begins with an invitation to praise, followed by reasons for praise.

Most of Psalm 100 is dedicated to the invitation to praise (verses 1-4). The reason for praise is succinctly stated in verse 5; God is good and God's love lasts forever. Just five verses long, Psalm 100 contains an important reminder. God is our God and deserves our praise. What a great reason to be joyful!

Spiritual Practice for Adults

Find some time to praise God through singing! Put on your favorite song and belt it out.

Come Together

Come Together

Supplies: Class Pack, Celebrate Wonder Bible Storybook, *Wonder Box, green cloth, battery-operated candle, bird*

Prepare Ahead: Set up a Wonder Table (see p. 3) with a green cloth, battery-operated candle, and a Wonder Box (see p. 3). Display the Unit 2 Bible Verse Poster (Class Pack—pp. 12 & 13) and Faith Word Poster (Class Pack—p. 4). Place the bird inside the Wonder Box.

- Point to the Unit 2 Faith Word Poster (Class Pack—p. 4), and invite the children to wonder about what the word *praise* means.

- Invite the kids to join you in a circle.

SAY: This month we will hear stories about praising God. This week we will read a psalm (a special song) all about making joyful noise as a way to praise God.

WONDER: What do you think a joyful noise is?

- In this curriculum, we recommend reading stories from the *Celebrate Wonder Bible Storybook.* Allow an elementary-age child to read the story, "Shout With Joy" (pp. 114–15) from the storybook.

PRAY: Dear God, we are so grateful for you and all of our blessings. Amen.

Shout With Joy – Preschool

Supplies: Reproducible Kids' Book, crayons

Prepare Ahead: Photocopy "Shout With Joy" (Reproducible 6A) for each child.

- Invite the preschoolers to use crayons to color the picture.

SAY: We can praise God with shouts of joy.

ASK: How else can you praise God?

Coded Message – Younger Elementary

Supplies: Reproducible Kids' Book, crayons

Prepare: Photocopy "Coded Message" (Reproducible 6B) for each child.

- Hand out a copy of "Coded Message" to each child.

SAY: Praise is the many ways we say thank you to God.

ASK: What is one way you can praise God?

SAY: Solve the coded message to find out!

- Invite the kids to solve the coded message.

Joyful – Older Elementary

Supplies: Reproducible Kids' Book, pens or pencils

Prepare Ahead: Photocopy "Joyful" (Reproducible 6C) for each child.

- Hand out a copy of "Joyful" to each child.

SAY: The Book of Psalms has lots of poems and songs in it that help us praise and worship God. One of the songs is Psalm 100. It encourages us to shout with joy.

ASK: What makes you joyful?

- Invite the kids to write one thing they are thankful for beside each letter on their worksheet.

- Encourage the kids to share their acrostic poems with the group.

Joyful Scavenger Hunt – All Ages

Supplies: Reproducible Kids' Book, crayons or markers

Prepare Ahead: Photocopy "Joyful Scavenger Hunt" (Reproducible 6D) for each child.

- Hand out copies of "Joyful Scavenger Hunt" (Reproducible 6D) to each child.

SAY: Find an item in the church that bring you joy that falls into each of the categories on your worksheet.

- Invite the kids to search for items in each category that brings them joy.

ASK: Why do these items bring you joy?

Wonder Time

Interactive Bible Story

Supplies: Reproducible Kids' Book

Prepare Ahead: Photocopy "Shout With Joy" (Reproducible 6F) for each child.

- Invite several readers to take turns reading the story one section at a time.

WONDER: Why do you think God wants us to shout with joy instead of whisper, or speak, or something else?

Share a Story

Supplies: Celebrate Wonder DVD, TV, DVD player

- Invite the children to join you and to sit in a circle on the floor.

- Watch the Session 6 video (Celebrate Wonder DVD).

Wonder with Me

Supplies: Class Pack, Wonder Box, scissors

Prepare Ahead: Lay out the Wonder Story Mat for Unit 2 (Class Pack—pp. 8 & 17). Cut out the Bible story figures (Class Pack—p.19).

- Place the Wonder Box on the Unit 2 Wonder Story Mat.

- Show the children the Unit 2 Faith Word Poster (Class Pack—p. 4).

SAY: Today's faith word is *praise*. Praise is one of the many ways we thank God.

- Show the children this week's figure—a singer.

WONDER together:

    ❍ What makes you want to shout with joy?

    ❍ What are you thankful for?

    ❍ What is your favorite way to praise God?

- Place the figure on the Wonder Story Mat.

- Open the Wonder Box to reveal the bird

WONDER: Why do you think a bird is in the Wonder Box this week?

Experience Wonder

Grateful, Thankful, Joyful Fun

Supplies: a die

SAY: There is so much to be grateful, thankful, and joyful about! We're going to play a game to helps us stare the things that bring us the feelings of being grateful, thankful, or joyful.

- Invite the kids to take turns rolling the die.

- If the kid rolls a one, they will share the name of someone in their lives that brings them joy.

- If the kid rolls a two, they will share about a place they are thankful for.

- If the kid rolls a three, they will share the name of a friend they are grateful for.
- If the kid rolls a four, they will share the name of activity in their lives that brings them joy.
- If the kid rolls a five, they will share about a book they are thankful for.
- If the kid rolls a six, they will share about a time they felt grateful for church.
- Give every child a chance to roll the die.
- Continue playing until the group is ready to move on.

SAY: There is so much in our lives that we can shout with joy about!

Examine the Bible Verse

SAY: Our Unit 2 Bible verse is Psalm 150:6. Find it in your Bibles.

ASK: Is Psalms in the Old or New Testament? *(Old)* Where is the Book of Psalms located in the Old Testament? *(nineteenth book, almost exactly in the center of the Bible)* In what chapter of Psalms is our verse located? *(150)* What is the verse number? *(6)*

SAY: Our Bible verse is all about praising God!

ASK: What's your favorite way to praise God?

- Gather the kids around the Bible Verse Poster (Class Pack—pp. 12 & 13). Read it together.

Peaceful Place

Supplies: *Leader Guide—p. 114, Celebrate Wonder Bible Storybook, book: The Thank You Book, by Mo Willems; music; paper; crayons or markers*

Prepare Ahead: *Photocopy the Unit 2 Faith Word coloring sheet (Leader Guide—p. 114) for each child.*

- Assist the children, as needed, as they interact with the items provided.
- Invite the children to explore music and singing.
- Have each child color the Faith Word coloring sheet.

Tip: *All of the supplies/activities suggested for the Peaceful Place are optional.*

Go in Peace

Spiritual Practice – Exploring Praise Through Worship

SAY: A spiritual practice is something we do to help us be present with God. A spiritual practice can be anything because you can be with God any time, anywhere, and any way! This month we are going to praise God through gratitude.

- Guide the children through a spiritual practice:
  - ○ **SAY:** We're going to think about five things we're grateful for. You'll close your eyes and I will say a place. You will think of something you are thankful for at that place.
  - ○ **SAY:** Get comfortable and close your eyes.
  - ○ **SAY:** At home, I am grateful for…
  - ○ **SAY:** At school, I am grateful for…
  - ○ **SAY:** In nature, I am grateful for…
  - ○ **SAY:** At church, I am grateful for…
  - ○ **SAY:** At the park, I am grateful for….

SAY: We can praise God for all of the things we are grateful for.

ASK: Would any of you like to share what you are grateful for?

PRAY: Repeat after me: "God, thank you for our many blessings. Help us always be ready to praise you. Amen."

- Bless the children before they leave. Touch each child on the hand as you say this blessing: "May you feel God's love all around you every day."

Family Spiritual Practice

Supplies: Reproducible Kids' Book; Leader Guide—pp. 111, 112

Prepare Ahead: Photocopy "Celebration Chart" (p. 111) and "Family Letter" (p. 112) for each child.

SAY: Let's take a look at your Take-Home Pages (*Reproducibles 6F–6G*). Ask your family to read the Bible story and participate in this week's spiritual devotion with you. There's an extra activity for you to do sometime this week.

- Send home a copy of the Take-Home Pages, a copy of the Family Letter, and a copy of the Celebration Chart with each child.

Supplemental Activities

Preschoolers and Early Elementary– Joyful Noises

Supplies: none

SAY: Let's use our voices to make joyful sounds to God. I will name a way to make a joyful noise and you'll say, "Praise God!" in the way I name. Ready?

SAY: Shout to the Lord!

- Invite the kids to shout, "Praise God!"

SAY: Whisper to the Lord!

- Invite the kids to whisper, "Praise God!"

SAY: Laugh to the Lord!

- Invite the kids to laugh the words, "Praise God!"

SAY: Sing to the Lord!

- Invite the kids to sing, "Praise God!"

SAY: Talk to the Lord!

- Invite the kids to say, "Praise God!"

SAY: Shout to the Lord!

- Invite the kids to shout, "Praise God!"

- Continue playing until the group is ready to move on.

Older Elementary – Thankful Jars

Supplies: 16-ounce mason jars, lots of paint pens, slips of paper, pens

SAY: Sometimes life gets hard, but there are always things we can be thankful for. We're going to decorate a mason jar using paint pens. Make a design that brings you joy! Then you will take the jar home and fill it with small slips of paper you've written your joys on.

- Give each child a mason jar.
- Invite the kids to decorate their jars with a design that brings them joy using paint pens.
- Give each child a slip of paper and a pen.
- Encourage them to write down something they are thankful for onto a slip of paper.
- Invite the kids to put their slips of paper into their jars.

Intergenerational Activity – Sing Together

Supplies: Reproducible Kids' Book

Prepare Ahead: *Photocopy "Shout to the Lord" (Reproducible 5E) for each participant.*

SAY: There is a song that was written based on Psalm 100 called "Shout to the Lord." Let's sing it together.

- Give each participant a copy of the words to the song "Shout to the Lord."
- Practice the chorus together a few times so your nonreaders and early readers can participate.
- Sing the song together.

ASK: What is your favorite song to sing to God?

PRAY: Dear God, thank you for our blessings. Hear our shouts of joy, our giggles of joy, and our silent joy. Amen.

Let every living thing praise the Lord! Praise the Lord! (Psalm 150:6)

Praise the Lord – Psalm 150

Prepare to Wonder

Faith Word: PRAISE

The Book of Psalms is an incredible book of Hebrew poetry. There are poems that express great gratitude and praise to God, but that's not all that's in the Psalter. The Psalter contains several genres: prayers for help and lament (both for individuals and communities), hymns of praise to be sung in worship, songs of thanksgiving for individuals and communities, instructional psalms, royal psalms relating to the king, and liturgies used in worship at the temple.

The Psalter could be read as one whole book or is divided into five books. If we side with The New Interpreter's One-Volume Commentary on the Bible, then the five books are Book I (1–41), Book II (42–72), Book III (73–89), Book IV (90–106), and Book V (107–150).

Psalm 150 is the Closing Doxology of Book V and of the entire Book of Psalms. If you were to read the Book of Psalms from Chapter 1 through Chapter 150, you'd conclude the experience is that of moving from lament to praise, both individualy and in community. What we see in many of the psalms is praise and thanksgiving for all that God has done and will do for the people of God. Psalm 100 tells every being to praise God in every way and with every kind of music.

Spiritual Practice for Adults

Find some time to praise God through playing music! You don't have to be a musician to play music either. Whether you have an instrument or you make a beat by clapping, playing music is one way of expressing praise.

Come Together

Come Together

Supplies: *Class Pack*, Celebrate Wonder Bible Storybook, *Wonder Box, green cloth, battery-operated candle, musical instrument*

Prepare Ahead: *Set up a Wonder Table (see p. 3) with a green cloth, battery-operated candle, and a Wonder Box (see p. 3). Display the Unit 2 Bible Verse Poster (Class Pack—pp. 12 & 13) and Faith Word Poster (Class Pack—p. 4). Place the musical instrument inside the Wonder Box.*

- Point to the Unit 2 Faith Word Poster (Class Pack—p. 4), and invite the children to wonder about what the word *praise* means.

- Invite the kids to join you in a circle.

SAY: This month we will hear stories about praising God. This week we will read a psalm (a special song) all about playing different instruments to praise God.

ASK: Do you know how to play an instrument? Is there an instrument you'd like to learn to play?

- In this curriculum, we recommend reading stories from the *Celebrate Wonder Bible Storybook.* Allow an elementary-age child to read the stories, "Praise the Lord" (pp. 116–117) from the storybook.

PRAY: Dear God, we are so grateful for you and all of our blessings. Amen.

Praise the Lord – Preschool

Supplies: *Reproducible Kids' Book, crayons*

Prepare Ahead: *Photocopy "Praise the Lord" (Reproducible 7A) for each child.*

- Invite the preschoolers to use crayons to color the picture.

SAY: We can praise God by playing music.

ASK: How else can you praise God?

Dot to Dot – Younger Elementary

Supplies: Reproducible Kids' Book, crayons

Prepare: Photocopy "Dot to Dot" (Reproducible 7B) for each child.

• Hand out a copy of "Dot to Dot" to each child.

SAY: Praise is one of the many ways we say thank you to God.

ASK: What is one way you can praise God?

SAY: The writer of Psalm 150 encourages everyone to praise God through music. Connect the dots to see how this person praises God through music.

• Invite the kids to connect the dots and then color the picture.

Song of Praise – Older Elementary

Supplies: Reproducible Kids' Book, pens or pencils

Prepare Ahead: Photocopy "Song of Praise" (Reproducible 7C) for each child.

• Hand out a copy of "Song of Praise" to each child.

SAY: The writer of psalm 150 encourages everyone to praise God through music. The Jewish people would have sung Psalm 150 as a song of praise.

ASK: Can you write your own song of praise like the writer of Psalm 150?

• Invite the kids to write their own songs of praise.

• Encourage the kids to share their songs with the group.

Psalm 150:6 – All Ages

Supplies: Reproducible Kids' Book, crayons or markers

Prepare Ahead: Photocopy "Psalm 150:6" (Reproducible 7D) for each child.

• Hand out copies of "Psalm 150:6" (Reproducible 7D) to each child.

SAY: Take a deep breath, then color this picture while you pray.

• Invite the kids to color the picture while they pray.

PRAY: Dear God, we are so grateful for our family—chosen and given, for our friends, and for our pets. We are so grateful for food and a safe place to sleep. Help us make sure everyone has food and a safe place to sleep. Amen.

Wonder Time

Interactive Bible Story

Supplies: *Reproducible Kids' Book*

Prepare Ahead: *Photocopy "Praise the Lord" (Reproducible 7F) for each child.*

• Invite several readers to take turns reading the story one section at a time.

WONDER: What is your favorite instrument?

Share a Story

Supplies: *Celebrate Wonder DVD, TV, DVD player*

• Invite the children to join you and to sit in a circle on the floor.

• Watch the Session 7 video (Celebrate Wonder DVD).

Wonder with Me

Supplies: *Class Pack, Wonder Box, scissors*

Prepare Ahead: *Lay out the Wonder Story Mat for Unit 2 (Class Pack—pp. 8 & 17). Cut out the Bible story figures (Class Pack—p.19).*

• Place the Wonder Box on the Unit 2 Wonder Story Mat.

• Show the children the Unit 2 Faith Word Poster (Class Pack—p. 4).

SAY: Today's faith word is *praise*. Praise is one of the many ways we thank God.

• Show the children this week's figure—a musician.

WONDER together:

    ❍ What kind of music makes you feel like praising God?

    ❍ What are you thankful for?

    ❍ What is your favorite way to praise God?

• Place the figure on the Wonder Story Mat.

• Open the Wonder Box to reveal the music instrument.

WONDER: Why do you think a music instrument is in the Wonder Box this week?

Experience Wonder

Match the Rhythm

Supplies: none

SAY: Praise is one of the many ways we say thank you to God. One of the ways we can praise God is through playing music. Let's make some music with our bodies!

- Invite the kids to sit in a circle.
- Encourage them to follow your rhythm. Pat your knees. Once they have that down, do a pat, pat, snap, pat, pat snap.
- Choose another child to make up a rhythm.
- After the mirroring the first child's rhythm, choose another.
- Continue playing until the group is ready to move on.

ASK: What is your favorite music?

Examine the Bible Verse

SAY: Our Unit 2 Bible verse is Psalm 150:6. Find it in your Bibles.

ASK: Is Psalms in the Old or New Testament? *(Old)* Where is the Book of Psalms located in the Old Testament? *(nineteenth book, almost exactly in the center of the Bible)* In what chapter of Psalms is our verse located? *(150)* What is the verse number? *(6)*

SAY: Our Bible verse is all about praising God!

ASK: What's your favorite way to praise God?

- Gather the kids around the Bible Verse Poster (Class Pack—pp. 12 & 13). Read it together.

Peaceful Place

Supplies: Leader Guide—p. 114, Celebrate Wonder Bible Storybook, book: The Giving Tree, by Shel Silverstein; musical instruments; paper; crayons or markers

Prepare Ahead: Photocopy the Unit 2 Faith Word coloring sheet (Leader Guide—p. 114) for each child.

- Assist the children, as needed, as they interact with the items provided.
- Invite the children to explore instruments.
- Have each child color the Faith Word coloring sheet.

Tip: All of the supplies/activities suggested for the Peaceful Place are optional.

Go in Peace

Spiritual Practice – Exploring Praise Through Worship

SAY: A spiritual practice is something we do to help us be present with God. A spiritual practice can be anything because you can be with God any time, anywhere, and any way! This month we are going to praise God through gratitude.

- Guide the children through a spiritual practice:
  - ○ **SAY:** We're going to think about five things we're grateful for. You'll close your eyes and I will say a place. You will think of something you are thankful for at that place.
  - ○ **SAY:** Get comfortable and close your eyes.
  - ○ **SAY:** At home, I am grateful for…
  - ○ **SAY:** At school, I am grateful for…
  - ○ **SAY:** In nature, I am grateful for…
  - ○ **SAY:** At church, I am grateful for…
  - ○ **SAY:** At the park, I am grateful for…

SAY: We can praise God for all of the things we are grateful for.

ASK: Would any of you like to share what you are grateful for?

PRAY: Repeat after me: "God, thank you for our many blessings. Help us always be ready to praise you. Amen."

- Bless the children before they leave. Touch each child on the hand as you say this blessing: "May you feel God's love all around you every day."

Family Spiritual Practice

Supplies: Reproducible Kids' Book; Leader Guide—pp. 111, 112

Prepare Ahead: Photocopy "Celebration Chart" (p. 111) and "Family Letter" (p. 112) for each child.

SAY: Let's take a look at your Take-Home Pages (*Reproducibles 7F–7G*). Ask your family to read the Bible story and participate in this week's spiritual devotion with you. There's an extra activity for you to do sometime this week.

- Send home a copy of the Take-Home Pages, a copy of the Family Letter, and a copy of the Celebration Chart with each child.

Supplemental Activities

Preschoolers – Jingle Bell Shaker Bracelet

Supplies: jingle bells, chenille stems

SAY: Praise is one of the many ways we say thank you to God. One way we can praise God is through playing music. Let's make some jingle bell shaker bracelets!

- Give each child a chenille stem and five jingle bells.
- Invite the kids to string the bells onto the chenille stem.
- Help the kids twist the ends together to make a bracelet.
- Encourage the kids to put on their bracelets and make some music.

Early Elementary– Paper Plate Shaker

Supplies: Reproducible Kids' Book, paper plates, pony beads, stapler, glue, crayons, scissors

Prepare Ahead: Photocopy "Shaker Decoration" (Reproducible 7E) for each child.

SAY: Praise is one of the many ways we say thank you to God. One way we can praise God is through playing music. Let's make some paper plate shakers!

- Give each kid a copy of "Shaker Decoration" to color.
- Invite the kids to color the picture and then cut it out.
- Give each child two paper plates with a handful of pony beads in the bottom plate.
- Place the other plate on top so there is a pocket of space in the middle of the plates. Help the kids staple the plates together.
- Help the kids glue their "Shaker Decoration" onto the top paper plate.
- Encourage the kids to shake the instrument to make some music.

Older Elementary – Mixed Media Instrument

Supplies: clean recyclables

SAY: Praise is one of the many ways we say thank you to God. One of the ways we can praise God is through playing music. Let's make some instruments from recycled materials!

- Invite the kids to make their own instruments using recycled materials.
- Encourage them to be creative.
- Invite the kids to show off their creations.

Intergenerational Activity – Name That Tune Game

Supplies: none

SAY: Praise is one of the many ways we say thank you to God. One way we can praise God is through playing music. Let's see if we can guess the names of some famous songs.

- Invite the participants to guess the song you hum.
- Hum the song "Amazing Grace."
- The participant who guesses correctly gets to hum the next song. If the group cannot guess the song, help the participant.
- Continue playing until everyone is ready to move on.

ASK: What is your favorite song to praise God?

PRAY: Dear God, thank you for our blessings. Amen.

Let every living thing praise the Lord! Praise the Lord! (Psalm 150:6)

Mary's Song – Luke 1:46-55

Prepare to Wonder

Faith Word: PRAISE

The gospel of Luke begins with the announcements of two upcoming births. The first announcement is to Elizabeth and Zechariah. The second birth announcement in Luke is the story of Gabriel telling Mary she will give birth to God's son. Gabriel also tells Mary her cousin Elizabeth is expecting a baby. The two story lines merge when Mary goes to visit Elizabeth.

When Elizabeth hears Mary's greeting, her child leapt in her womb. Elizabeth tells Mary the baby jumped for joy in the presence of the Lord. There is no indication Elizabeth knew of Mary's pregnancy prior to her visit. When her baby jumped for joy, Elizabeth takes this as a sign. Elizabeth's baby, who grows up to become John the Baptist, identifies Jesus as Lord even when they are both still in the womb.

Upon seeing Mary, Elizabeth is filled with the Holy Spirit and makes several pronouncements. She tells Mary God has blessed her and the child she carries. Elizabeth also questions why she has been given the honor of the Lord visiting her. Even though an angel had told Mary she was pregnant with God's son, it must have been reassuring to receive this affirmation from Elizabeth. Following Elizabeth's greeting, Mary makes a joyful response of her own, praising God with a song that has become known as the Magnificat. Mary recalled God's actions in the past and trusted in God to continue to be at work in her life. God is at work in each of our lives as well. Remembering God is at work in our lives helps us respond with joy.

Spiritual Practice for Adults

Find some time to praise God through poetry. You could read a psalm, a poem by a favorite poet, or listen to a song or a poetry podcast, like Poetry Unbound. Mary's Magnificant is a poem. How is God speaking to you in the poem?

Come Together

Come Together

Supplies: Class Pack, Celebrate Wonder Bible Storybook, *Wonder Box, green cloth, battery-operated candle, poem*

Prepare Ahead: Set up a Wonder Table (see p. 3) with a green cloth, battery-operated candle, and a Wonder Box (see p. 3). Display the Unit 2 Bible Verse Poster (Class Pack—pp. 12 & 13) and Faith Word Poster (Class Pack—p. 4). Place the poem inside the Wonder Box.

- Point to the Unit 2 Faith Word Poster (Class Pack—p. 4), and invite the children to wonder about what the word *praise* means.

- Invite the kids to join you in a circle.

SAY: This month we will hear stories about praising God. This week we will read a poem that Mary, Jesus' mom, sang to praise God.

ASK: What do you like to do when you want to praise God?

- In this curriculum, we recommend reading stories from the *Celebrate Wonder Bible Storybook*. Allow an elementary-age child to read the story, "Mary's Song" (pp. 196–97) from the storybook.

PRAY: Dear God, we are so grateful for you and all of our blessings. Amen.

Mary's Song – Preschool

Supplies: Reproducible Kids' Book, crayons

Prepare Ahead: Photocopy "Mary's Song" (Reproducible 8A) for each child.

- Invite the preschoolers to use crayons to color the picture.

SAY: When Mary, Jesus' mom, found out she was going to have a baby, she sang a song of praise to God.

ASK: What would you sing about?

What Doesn't Belong? – Younger Elementary

Supplies: Reproducible Kids' Book, crayons

Prepare: Photocopy "What Doesn't Belong?" (Reproducible 8B) for each child.

• Hand out a copy of "What Doesn't Belong?" to each child.

SAY: When Mary, Jesus' mom, found out she was going to have a baby, she sang a song of praise to God.

ASK: Can you find the things that don't belong?

SAY: Circle them and then color the picture.

• Invite the kids to find and circle the things that don't belong, and then color the picture.

Word Search – Older Elementary

Supplies: Reproducible Kids' Book, pens or pencils

Prepare Ahead: Photocopy "Word Search" (Reproducible 8C) for each child.

• Hand out a copy of "Word Search" to each child.

SAY: When Mary, Jesus' mom, found out she was going to have a baby, she sang a song of praise to God.

ASK: What would you sing about?

• Invite the kids to circle the words in the puzzle.

Memory Verse Art – All Ages

Supplies: Reproducible Kids' Book, scissors, glue, construction paper, crayons or markers

Prepare Ahead: Photocopy "Memory Verse Art" (Reproducible 8D) for each child.

• Hand out copies of "Memory Verse Art" (Reproducible 8D) to each child.

• Give each kids a copy of Reproducible 8D.

• Invite the kids to color the words and then cut them out.

• Give each child a piece of construction paper.

• Encourage them to create art by gluing the memory verse words onto the construction paper. Then, have them decorate their papers with markers.

WONDER: What would it look like for a dog to praise God? Or a tree?

Wonder Time

Interactive Bible Story

Supplies: Reproducible Kids' Book

Prepare Ahead: Photocopy "Mary's Song" (Reproducible 8F) for each child.

• Invite several readers to take turns reading the story one section at a time.

WONDER: What is your favorite part of Mary's song?

Share a Story

Supplies: Celebrate Wonder DVD, TV, DVD player

• Invite the children to join you and to sit in a circle on the floor.

• Watch the Session 8 video (Celebrate Wonder DVD).

Wonder with Me

Supplies: Class Pack, Wonder Box, scissors

Prepare Ahead: Lay out the Wonder Story Mat for Unit 2 (Class Pack—pp. 8 & 17). Cut out the Bible story figures (Class Pack—p.19).

• Place the Wonder Box on the Unit 2 Wonder Story Mat.

• Show the children the Unit 2 Faith Word Poster (Class Pack—p. 4).

SAY: Today's faith word is *praise*. Praise is one of the many ways we thank God.

• Show the children this week's figure—a poet.

WONDER together:

    ◯ What is your favorite poem?

    ◯ What are you thankful for?

    ◯ What is your favorite way to praise God?

    ◯ What has God done in your life?

• Place the figure on the Wonder Story Mat.

• Open the Wonder Box to reveal the poem.

WONDER: Why do you think a poem is in the Wonder Box this week?

Experience Wonder

Christmas in July

Supplies: Reproducible Kids' Book, construction paper, crayons or markers, scissors, glue sticks

Prepare Ahead: Photocopy "Christmas in July" (Reproducible 8E) for each child.

SAY: We usually only hear about Mary at Christmas time when we are preparing for the birth of Jesus. Let's celebrate Christmas in July! Jesus' birth is always worthy of praise.

- Give each child a copy of Reproducible 8E.
- Invite the kids to color the figures.
- Help them cut out the nativity figures.
- Encourage them to arrange and glue their nativity figures on the construction paper.
- Invite them to draw a stable or guestroom to put the figures in.

ASK: What is your favorite Christmas memory?

Examine the Bible Verse

SAY: Our Unit 2 Bible verse is Psalm 150:6. Find it in your Bibles.

ASK: Is Psalms in the Old or New Testament? *(Old)* Where is the Book of Psalms located in the Old Testament? *(nineteenth book, almost exactly in the center of the Bible)* In what chapter of Psalms is our verse located? *(150)* What is the verse number? *(6)*

SAY: Our Bible verse is all about praising God!

ASK: What's your favorite way to praise God?

- Gather the kids around the Bible Verse Poster (Class Pack—pp. 12 & 13). Read it together.

Peaceful Place

Supplies: Leader Guide—p. 114, Celebrate Wonder Bible Storybook, *book:* 'Twas the Evening of Christmas, *by Glenys Nellist; nativity play set; paper; crayons or markers*

Prepare Ahead: Photocopy the Unit 2 Faith Word coloring sheet (Leader Guide—p. 114) for each child.

- Assist the children, as needed, as they interact with the items provided.
- Invite the children to explore the nativity.
- Have each child color the Faith Word coloring sheet.

Tip: All of the supplies/activities suggested for the Peaceful Place are optional.

Go in Peace

Spiritual Practice – Exploring Praise Through Worship.

SAY: A spiritual practice is something we do to help us be present with God. A spiritual practice can be anything because you can be with God any time, anywhere, and any way! This month we are going to praise God through gratitude.

- Guide the children through a spiritual practice:

  ○ **SAY:** We're going to think about five things we're grateful for. You'll close your eyes and I will say a place. You will think of something you are thankful for at that place.

  ○ **SAY:** Get comfortable and close your eyes.

  ○ **SAY:** At home, I am grateful for…

  ○ **SAY:** At school, I am grateful for…

  ○ **SAY:** In nature, I am grateful for…

  ○ **SAY:** At church, I am grateful for…

  ○ **SAY:** At the park, I am grateful for…

SAY: We can praise God for all of the things we are grateful for.

ASK: Would any of you like to share what you are grateful for?

PRAY: Repeat after me: "God, thank you for our many blessings. Help us always be ready to praise you. Amen."

- Bless the children before they leave. Touch each child on the hand as you say this blessing: "May you feel God's love all around you every day."

Family Spiritual Practice

Supplies: Reproducible Kids' Book; Leader Guide—pp. 111, 112

Prepare Ahead: Photocopy "Celebration Chart" (p. 111) and "Family Letter" (p. 112) for each child.

SAY: Let's take a look at your Take-Home Pages (*Reproducibles 8F–8G*). Ask your family to read the Bible story and participate in this week's spiritual devotion with you. There's an extra activity for you to do sometime this week.

- Send home a copy of the Take-Home Pages, a copy of the Family Letter, and a copy of the Celebration Chart with each child.

Supplemental Activities

Preschoolers – Praise Walk

SAY: Praise is one of the many ways we say thank you to God.

ASK: What is one thing you are thankful for today?

SAY: Let's go on a walk and see what other things we are thankful for.

- Invite the kids to follow you as you walk around the room and encourage the kids to point out things that we can be thankful for.
- If able, repeat this activity around the inside of the church building and outside.

Early Elementary– Praise Chain

Supplies: *construction paper, markers, stapler, scissors*

Prepare Ahead: *Cut the construction paper into 1-inch strips.*

SAY: Praise is one of the many ways we say thank you to God. Let's make a praise chain to see how many things we're thankful for.

- Give each kid a few strips.
- Invite the kids to write or draw one thing they are thankful for on each strip.
- Help each kid make a loop with one strip and staple it into a circle.
- Help each kid thread a second strip through the loop and make another loop.
- Encourage them to keep making loops until they have a chain.
- Invite the kids to share their chains with the group.

Older Elementary – Emotions of Praise

Supplies: card stock, watercolor paints, paintbrushes, cups of water

SAY: Praise is one of the many ways we say thank you to God.

WONDER: How does praise feel?

SAY: We're going to paint what praise feels like with watercolors. Your painting doesn't have to be of anything. It can just be the colors that you think the feeling of praise would look like.

- Give each child a piece of card stock and a paintbrush.
- Invite the kids to paint what praise feels like with watercolors.
- Set the painting somewhere to dry.
- Once the paintings are dry, invite the kids to show off their paintings.

Intergenerational Activity – Praise Poem

Supplies: paper, pens or pencils

SAY: Mary praised God through a poetic song. Let's write poetic songs!

- Divide the participants into groups of four.
- Invite the participants to write poems about praise. They can be funny or serious or triumphant, like Mary's poem.
- Encourage the groups to share their poems.

ASK: What is your favorite way to praise God?

PRAY: Dear God, thank you for our blessings. Amen.

Let every living thing praise the LORD! Praise the LORD! (Psalm 150:6)

Salt and Light – Matthew 5:13-16

Prepare to Wonder

Faith Word: PRAISE

This week's Scripture comes from Jesus' Sermon on the Mount found in Matthew 5–7. These chapters are some of Jesus' core teachings and have been studied by many scholars trying to understand better what a life following Jesus should look like.

Jesus begins his teachings on the mount with what has come to be known as the Beatitudes. Right after these verses comes today's passage often referred to as "Salt and Light." Matthew 5:13-16 can be broken into two parts—5:13 and 5:14-16. Verse 5:13 is about salt and verses 5:14-16 are about light.

Salt is a chemical compound of sodium and chloride, and is an extremely stable compound. That means it's very hard to break down and salt cannot lose its flavor. The only way something can lose its saltiness is by being mixed with so many other things that its saltiness is hidden. Salt can only be salt. If salt has be compromised so much that it is no longer salty, it is no longer salt. Jesus is trying to remind his followers that we are to live a life of authenticity and to not lose what makes us unique.

Light helps us see. We don't really see light, we see what light shows us. Jesus is encouraging the followers to live a life that shows others his love. Jesus encourages the followers to shine bright for all to see.

Spiritual Practice for Adults

Find some time to praise God through writing. Here is a writing prompt: what makes you who you are? What about you is unique?

Come Together

Come Together

Supplies: *Class Pack,* Celebrate Wonder Bible Storybook, *Wonder Box, green cloth, battery-operated candle, flashlight*

Prepare Ahead: *Set up a Wonder Table (see p. 3) with a green cloth, battery-operated candle, and a Wonder Box (see p. 3). Display the Unit 2 Bible Verse Poster (Class Pack—pp. 12 & 13) and Faith Word Poster (Class Pack—p. 4). Place the flashlight inside the Wonder Box.*

- Point to the Unit 2 Faith Word Poster (Class Pack—p. 4), and invite the children to wonder about what the word *praise* means.
- Invite the kids to join you in a circle.

SAY: This month we will hear stories about praising God. This week we will read a teaching of Jesus called, "Salt and Light."

WONDER: What do you think salt and light have to do with praising God?

- In this curriculum, we recommend reading stories from the *Celebrate Wonder Bible Storybook.* Allow an elementary-age child to read the story, "Salt and Light" (pp. 148–149) from the storybook.

PRAY: Dear God, we are so grateful for you and all of our blessings. Amen.

Salt and Light – Preschool

Supplies: *Reproducible Kids' Book, crayons*

Prepare Ahead: *Photocopy "Salt and Light" (Reproducible 9A) for each child.*

- Invite the preschoolers to use crayons to color the picture.

SAY: Jesus told a story about salt and light. He wanted to teach people how special they are and to encourage them to share that specialness with the whole world!

ASK: What makes you special?

Word Search – Younger Elementary

Supplies: *Reproducible Kids' Book, crayons*

Prepare: *Photocopy "Word Search" (Reproducible 9B) for each child.*

- Hand out a copy of "Word Search" to each child.

SAY: We heard lots of great stories about praise this month. Praise is the many ways we say thank you to God.

ASK: Which story was your favorite?

- Invite the kids to find and circle the words listed in the work bank.

Crossword – Older Elementary

Supplies: Reproducible Kids' Book, pens or pencils

Prepare Ahead: Photocopy "Crossword" (Reproducible 9C) for each child.

- Hand out a copy of "Crossword" to each child.

SAY: We heard lots of great stories about praise this month. Praise is the many ways we say thank you to God.

ASK: Which story was your favorite?

- Invite the kids to solve the puzzle.

July Stars and Constellations – All Ages

Supplies: Reproducible Kids' Book

Prepare Ahead: Photocopy "July Stars and Constellations" (Reproducible 9D) for each child.

- Hand out copies of Reproducible 9D.

- Invite the kids to look over the stars, constellations, and star pictures on the page.

ASK: Do you recognize any of the star pictures on the page?

- Invite the kids to share any star pictures they recognize. This sheet shows the same stars and constellations that we saw in May. Use this opportunity to see if any kids in your class have tried to find star pictures in the sky.

SAY: This fall, we began looking at the night sky to see star pictures. If you are having trouble finding these shapes, here's a tip.

- Point to Orion on the star chart.

SAY: Orion is the figure of a man. His belt has three bright stars that are pretty easy to find in the winter sky. If you can find the belt, you might be able to find some of the other stars and constellations on the sheet.

- Invite the kids to take the sheets home and look at the sky.

Wonder Time

Interactive Bible Story

Supplies: *Reproducible Kids' Book*

Prepare Ahead: *Photocopy "Salt and Light" (Reproducible 9F) for each child.*

• Invite several readers to take turns reading the story one section at a time.

WONDER: What things make you who you are?

Share a Story

Supplies: *Celebrate Wonder DVD, TV, DVD player*

• Invite the children to join you and to sit in a circle on the floor.

• Watch the Session 9 video (Celebrate Wonder DVD).

Wonder with Me

Supplies: *Class Pack, Wonder Box, scissors*

Prepare Ahead: *Lay out the Wonder Story Mat for Unit 2 (Class Pack—pp. 8 & 17). Cut out the Bible story figures (Class Pack—p.19).*

• Place the Wonder Box on the Unit 2 Wonder Story Mat.

• Show the children the Unit 2 Faith Word Poster (Class Pack—p. 4).

SAY: Today's faith word is *praise*. Praise is one of the many ways we thank God.

• Show the children this week's figure—a writer.

WONDER together:

❍ Why did Jesus talk about salt instead of something else?

❍ What are you thankful for?

❍ What is your favorite way to praise God?

• Place the figure on the Wonder Story Mat.

• Open the Wonder Box to reveal the flashlight.

WONDER: Why do you think a flashlight is in the Wonder Box this week?

Experience Wonder

Charades

Supplies: Reproducible Kids' Book, scissors, bowl

Prepare Ahead: Photocopy "Charades" (Reproducible 9E) and cut out the twelve cards. Place the cards in a bowl

SAY: We heard lots of great stories about praise this month. Praise is one of the many ways we say thank you to God.

ASK: Which story was your favorite?

SAY: We're going to take turns acting out the different ways we can praise God and guessing what type of praise it is.

- Invite one kid to draw a card from the bowl.
- Encourage the kid to act out that type of praise.
- Invite the other kids to guess what type of praise it is.
- Whoever guesses correctly gets to act out the next card.
- Continue playing in this way until your group has gone through all twelve cards.

ASK: What is your favorite way to praise God?

Examine the Bible Verse

SAY: Our Unit 2 Bible verse is Psalm 150:6. Find it in your Bibles.

ASK: Is Psalms in the Old or New Testament? *(Old)* Where is the Book of Psalms located in the Old Testament? *(nineteenth book, almost exactly in the center of the Bible)* In what chapter of Psalms is our verse located? *(150)* What is the verse number? *(6)*

SAY: Our Bible verse is all about praising God!

ASK: What's your favorite way to praise God?

- Gather the kids around the Bible Verse Poster (Class Pack—pp. 12 & 13). Read it together.

Peaceful Place

Supplies: *Leader Guide—p. 114,* Celebrate Wonder Bible Storybook, *book:* Llama Llama Gives Thanks, *by Anna Dewdney; paper; crayons or markers*

Prepare Ahead: *Photocopy the Unit 2 Faith Word coloring sheet (Leader Guide—p. 114) for each child.*

- Assist the children, as needed, as they interact with the items provided.
- Invite the children to draw a self-portrait.
- Have each child color the Faith Word coloring sheet.

Tip: *All of the supplies/activities suggested for the Peaceful Place are optional.*

Go in Peace

Spiritual Practice – Exploring Praise Through Worship.

SAY: A spiritual practice is something we do to help us be present with God. A spiritual practice can be anything because you can be with God any time, anywhere, and any way! This month we are going to praise God through gratitude.

- Guide the children through a spiritual practice:
  - ❍ **SAY:** We're going to think about five things we're grateful for. You'll close your eyes and I will say a place. You will think of something you are thankful for at that place.
  - ❍ **SAY:** Get comfortable and close your eyes.
  - ❍ **SAY:** At home, I am grateful for…
  - ❍ **SAY:** At school, I am grateful for…
  - ❍ **SAY:** In nature, I am grateful for…
  - ❍ **SAY:** At church, I am grateful for…
  - ❍ **SAY:** At the park, I am grateful for…

SAY: We can praise God for all of the things we are grateful for.

ASK: Would any of you like to share what you are grateful for?

PRAY: Repeat after me: "God, thank you for our many blessings. Help us always be ready to praise you. Amen."

- Bless the children before they leave. Touch each child on the hand as you say this blessing: "May you feel God's love all around you every day."

Family Spiritual Practice

Supplies: Reproducible Kids' Book; Leader Guide—pp. 111, 112

Prepare Ahead: Photocopy "Celebration Chart" (p. 111) and "Family Letter" (p. 112) for each child.

SAY: Let's take a look at your Take-Home Pages *(Reproducibles 9F–9G)*. Ask your family to read the Bible story and participate in this week's spiritual devotion with you. There's an extra activity for you to do sometime this week.

- Send home a copy of the Take-Home Pages, a copy of the Family Letter, and a copy of the Celebration Chart with each child.

Supplemental Activities

Preschoolers – This Little Light of Mine

SAY: Let's sing a song to help us remember our story from today!

- Invite the kids to sing with you.

SING: This little light of mine
I'm going to let it shine
This little light of mine
I'm going to let it shine
This little light of mine
I'm going to let it shine
Let it shine, all the time, let it shine

ALL around the neighborhood
I'm going to let it shine
All around the neighborhood
I'm going to let it shine
All around the neighborhood
I'm going to let it shine
Let it shine, all the time, let it shine.

HIDE it under a bushel? No!
I'm going to let it shine
Hide it under a bushel? No!
I'm going to let it shine
Hide it under a bushel? No!
I'm going to let it shine
Let it shine, all the time, let it shine.

Early Elementary and Older Elementary– Flashlight Tag

Supplies: flashlights, dim space

SAY: Jesus wants us to shine our light! Let's play flashlight tag to help us remember this teaching of Jesus.

- Choose one child to be it and give that child a flashlight.

- It will chose their eyes and count to 15. While they count, the rest of the group will find hiding spots.

- When it reaches 15, they will seek the hiders and tag them with the light of the flashlight.

- When a new child has been tagged, they become it and take the flashlight and goes to find other kids while the original it goes to hide.

- Continue playing until you are ready to move on.

Intergenerational Activity – Thank-You Cards

Supplies: scrapbook paper, card stock, pens or pencils, stickers, markers or crayons, scissors

SAY: This month we've talked a lot about praise and gratitude.

ASK: What are you thankful for?

ASK: Who are you thankful for?

SAY: We're going to make beautiful cards for someone we are thankful for.

- Invite the participants to make thank-you cards using the supplies provided.

- Encourage the participants to give or mail their cards to the people they are thankful for.

PRAY: Dear God, thank you for our blessings. Amen.

In the beginning was the Word and the Word was with God and the Word was God. (John 1:1)

Wise Writings –
Proverbs 6:6-8; 10:1; 17:17

Prepare to Wonder

Faith Word: SCRIPTURE

When Solomon became king, he prayed and asked God for wisdom. God granted Solomon's request and throughout Solomon's life he was known for having great wisdom. Many people came to Solomon to ask his advice.

The Book of Proverbs contains many of Solomon's wise sayings. Much of the book is attributed to Solomon though a couple of sections are considered to have been written by other people. A proverb is a short saying that imparts truth. Proverbs offer advice about many aspects of life. If we pay attention this wisdom can help us make good decisions and live as God wants us to live.

This week we look at several of the proverbs that will show us examples of Solomon's wisdom. King Solomon told a story about ants to teach people about working hard. Because ants work hard to gather food, they have sufficient food to eat. Ants are responsible without having a boss to tell them what to do. The tale of the ants is a lesson for human beings, warning against laziness.

Solomon's proverbs offer wisdom to family and friends alike. He offered advice on parents and their children, advising that parents are delighted when their children are wise and sad when they are foolish. On friends, Solomon offers the observation that friends are to love all the time.

Spiritual Practice for Adults

This month, we will try out the spiritual practice called *lectio divina*. It's a practice of reading Scripture out loud to hear what God might be saying to you through the passage. Read Proverbs 6:6-8; 10:1; 17:1. What stands out to you from these verses? Read Proverbs 6:6-8; 10:1; 17:1 again. What might God be telling you? Take time to write down what you are hearing from God in these verses.

Come Together

Come Together

Supplies: *Class Pack*, Celebrate Wonder Bible Storybook, *Wonder Box, green cloth, battery-operated candle, owl*

Prepare Ahead: *Set up a Wonder Table (see p. 3) with a green cloth, battery-operated candle, and a Wonder Box (see p. 3). Display the Unit 3 Bible Verse Poster (Class Pack—pp. 9 & 16) and Faith Word Poster (Class Pack—p. 21). Place the owl inside the Wonder Box.*

- Point to the Unit 3 Faith Word Poster (Class Pack—p. 21), and invite the children to wonder about what the word *Scripture* means.

- Invite the kids to join you in a circle.

SAY: This month we will hear stories about people who wrote passages in the Bible. This week we will read some of the writings King Solomon wrote in the Book of Proverbs. A proverb is a short saying that helps us make good choices.

WONDER: What is the best advice you've been given?

- In this curriculum, we recommend reading stories from the *Celebrate Wonder Bible Storybook*. Allow an elementary-age child to read the story, "Wise Writings" (pp. 118–19) from the storybook.

PRAY: Dear God, help us hear your love through the writings in our Bibles. Amen.

Wise Writings – Preschool

Supplies: *Reproducible Kids' Book, crayons*

Prepare Ahead: *Photocopy "Wise Writings" (Reproducible 10A) for each child.*

- Invite the preschoolers to use crayons to color the picture.

SAY: King Solomon was a wise king. He wrote down some of the advice he shared in the Book of Proverbs found in our Bible.

ASK: What advice would you share?

Hidden Word – Younger Elementary

Supplies: Reproducible Kids' Book, crayons

Prepare: Photocopy "Hidden Word" (Reproducible 10B) for each child.

• Hand out a copy of "Hidden Word" to each child.

SAY: King Solomon was a wise king. He wrote down some of the advice he shared in the Book of Proverbs found in our Bible.

ASK: Can you find the hidden letters in the picture? What word do the letters spell?

• Invite the kids to find and circle the hidden letters in the picture.

• Help them unscramble the word.

• Encourage them to color the picture.

Coded Message – Older Elementary

Supplies: Reproducible Kids' Book, pens or pencils

Prepare Ahead: Photocopy "Coded Message" (Reproducible 10C) for each child.

• Hand out a copy of "Coded Message" to each child.

SAY: This month we are learning about Scripture—God's living word. We are exploring Scripture through writing.

ASK: What is your favorite Scripture?

SAY: The coded verse is a favorite of a lot of people. Solve the puzzle to read it.

• Invite the kids to solve the puzzle.

Your Proverbs – All Ages

Supplies: Reproducible Kids' Book, crayons or markers

Prepare Ahead: Photocopy "Your Proverbs" (Reproducible 10D) for each child.

SAY: King Solomon was a wise king. He wrote down some of the advice he shared in the Book of Proverbs found in our Bible.

ASK: What advice would you share?

• Hand out copies of Reproducible 10D.

• Invite the kids to draw or write the best advice they have for their families or the church on the worksheet.

Wonder Time

Interactive Bible Story

Supplies: Reproducible Kids' Book

Prepare Ahead: Photocopy "Wise Writings" (Reproducible 10F) for each child.

- Invite several readers to take turns reading the story one section at a time.

WONDER: What makes these sayings wise?

Share a Story

Supplies: Celebrate Wonder DVD, TV, DVD player

- Invite the children to join you and to sit in a circle on the floor.
- Watch the Session 10 video (Celebrate Wonder DVD).

Wonder with Me

Supplies: Class Pack, Wonder Box, scissors

Prepare Ahead: Lay out the Wonder Story Mat for Unit 3 (Class Pack—pp. 7 & 18). Cut out the Bible story figures (Class Pack—p.3).

- Place the Wonder Box on the Unit 3 Wonder Story Mat.
- Show the children the Unit 3 Faith Word Poster (Class Pack—p. 21).

SAY: Today's faith word is *Scripture*. Scripture is God's living word.

- Show the children this week's figure—a scroll with Proverbs 17:17 on it.

WONDER together:

○ What other wise things have you learned from the Bible?

○ What makes a person wise?

○ Who is the wisest person you know?

- Place the figure on the Wonder Story Mat.
- Open the Wonder Box to reveal the owl.

WONDER: Why do you think an owl is in the Wonder Box this week?

Experience Wonder

Wisdom Books

Supplies: watercolor paints, paintbrushes, cups of water, card stock, index cards

Prepare Ahead: Before class, write the following books of the Bible onto index cards—Job, Proverbs, and Ecclesiastes.

SAY: Our Bible is a library of books. Just like at the library, there are different kinds of books. There are books about history, books of poetry, stories, and so much more.

ASK: What's your favorite kind of books?

SAY: We're hearing wise writings this month. This week and next week will read from two of the books that are a part of the wisdom books.

SAY: The wisdom books are Job, Proverbs, and Ecclesiastes. They are called wisdom books because they talk about what it means to be a wise and righteous person.

WONDER: What makes a person wise?

SAY: In our Bibles, there is no one way to be a wise person. The different books show us ways others have lived wisely.

- Invite the kids to paint a picture of a time when they made a wise choice.

- When they are finished painting, encourage them to share their pictures with the group.

ASK: What make this moment of wisdom stand out to you?

Examine the Bible Verse

SAY: Our Unit 3 Bible verse is John 1:1. Find it in your Bibles.

ASK: Is John in the Old or New Testament? *(New)* Where is the Book of John located in the New Testament? *(fourth book)* In what chapter of John is our verse located? *(1)* What is the verse number? *(1)*

SAY: Our Bible has lots of wise things to teach us!

WONDER: What does this verse teach you?

- Gather the kids around the Bible Verse Poster (Class Pack—pp. 9 & 16). Read it together.

Peaceful Place

Supplies: *Leader Guide—p. 115, Celebrate Wonder Bible Storybook, book: Knuffle Bunny, by Mo Willems; paper; crayons or markers*

Prepare Ahead: *Photocopy the Unit 3 Faith Word coloring sheet (Leader Guide—p. 115) for each child.*

• Assist the children, as needed, as they interact with the items provided.

• Have each child color the Faith Word coloring sheet.

Tip: *All of the supplies/activities suggested for the Peaceful Place are optional.*

Go in Peace

Spiritual Practice – Exploring Scripture Through Writing.

Supplies: *paper, pens or pencils*

SAY: A spiritual practice is something we do to help us be present with God. A spiritual practice can be anything because you can be with God any time, anywhere, and any way! This month we are going to connect with God through writing.

• Guide the children through a spiritual practice:

　❍ **SAY:** Writing down our thoughts and feelings can connect us to God. Let's take a deep breath. Close your eyes. Take a deep breath. What do you feel? Take a deep breath. What do you think? Take a deep breath. Open your eyes.

　❍ Give each child a piece of paper and encourage them to write (or draw) what they feel and think today.

　❍ **WONDER:** Where is God when we feel and think these things?

SAY: God is always with us and isn't scared of any of our thoughts or feelings.

ASK: Would any of you like to share what you are thinking and feeling?

PRAY: Repeat after me: "God, we are so glad you are always with us. Amen."

• Bless the children before they leave. Touch each child on the hand as you say this blessing: "May you feel God's love all around you every day."

Family Spiritual Practice

Supplies: Reproducible Kids' Book; Leader Guide—pp. 111, 112

Prepare Ahead: Photocopy "Celebration Chart" (p. 111) and "Family Letter" (p. 112) for each child.

SAY: Let's take a look at your Take-Home Pages *(Reproducibles 10F–10G)*. Ask your family to read the Bible story and participate in this week's spiritual devotion with you. There's an extra activity for you to do sometime this week.

• Send home a copy of the Take-Home Pages, a copy of the Family Letter, and a copy of the Celebration Chart with each child.

Supplemental Activities

Preschoolers – Ant Work Relay

Supplies: buckets or bowls, cotton balls

• Divide the kids into teams of four.

SAY: Let's pretend to be ants! We will pick up food (the cotton balls) and store the food in our buckets. Let's see which team can gather the most food!

• Give each team a bucket or bowl.

• Pour cotton balls out onto the floor.

• When you say go, encourage the kids to work together as a team to collect as many cotton balls as they can until all of the cotton balls have been picked up.

• Play several times until your group is ready to move on.

Early Elementary – Paper Plate Snow Owl

Supplies: white paper plates, black and brown markers, orange and yellow construction paper, scissors, stapler, glue

SAY: Owls have been a symbol of wisdom for a long time! Let's make a snow owl to remind us to be wise.

• Give each child a white paper plate.

• Encourage the kids to fold the paper plate in half and then unfold the plate.

• Have them fold the left edge to the center line. Have them fold the right edge to the center line. The plate will look a little like a burrito.

• Invite the kids to fold the top down to make the owls' heads. Add a staple at the center bottom edge of the folded down top to keep the owl together.

- Encourage the kids to use markers to create feathers by drawing a series of scalloped lines on the wings.

- Help each child cut out two yellow circles for eyes and one orange triangle for a beak. If you wish to include feet, help kids to trace simple feet for their owl.

- Invite the kids to glue the eyes and beak to their plate. The beak will cover the staple.

- Encourage the kids to add pupils to the owl's eyes with a black marker.

Older Elementary– King Solomon's Wisdom

Supplies: Bibles, paper, pencils or pens

SAY: Solomon asked for God's help to be king. He wanted to be able to know the difference between right and wrong. God gave Solomon wisdom and he became well-known for his wise sayings. We've heard some of Solomon's wisdom today.

- Have the children find the Book of Proverbs in their Bibles.

- Give each kid a Bible, a piece of paper, and a pencil.

SAY: Look up Proverbs 6:6-8; 10:1; 17:17. Read the proverb and think about what it means. Then rewrite the proverb in your own words.

- Allow time for children to reflect and write. Let children work in pairs or individually.

- After the children have finished, review the proverbs together.

ASK: What makes these sayings wise?

Intergenerational Activity – Is It Wise?

Supplies: Reproducible Kids' Book

Prepare Ahead: Photocopy "Is It Wise?" (Reproducible 10E) for each participant.

SAY: Solomon asked God for wisdom to help him make good choices. We can make good and wise choices too. Let's decide if these things are wise and good. If they aren't wise, what should we do instead?

- Invite the participants to take turns reading the statements out loud.

- After each statement is read, ask the participants if the statement is wise. If it isn't a wise choice, what would they do instead?

- Encourage the participants to talk about why something is or isn't wise.

PRAY: Dear God, thank you for wisdom. Help us make good and wise choices. Amen.

In the beginning was the Word and the Word was with God and the Word
was God. (John 1:1)

Everything Has a Season –
Ecclesiastes 3:1-8

Prepare to Wonder

Faith Word: SCRIPTURE

The Book of Ecclesiastes is part of the Wisdom writings in the Old Testament. Unlike
Proverbs and Job, the writer of Ecclesiastes has a cynical perspective on life. The writer
is wrestling with the hard realities of life and wondering what makes life worth living.
We don't know who the writer is, but some scholars attribute the book to the wise king,
Solomon. We do know that the writer is hoping to impart wisdom to the reader.

The passage of Ecclesiastes that we will read is the most quoted part of this book.
The poetry of Ecclesiastes 3:1-8 has inspired readers (and songwriters) for a long
time. These verses remind the reader that we are not in control of much, but we can
trust that God is knitting together the seasons of our lives. There will be times of joy,
times of grief, times of boredom, times of success, and times for moving on. In all of
these moments, God is with us.

Spiritual Practice for Adults

This month, we will try out the spiritual practice called *lectio divina*. It's a practice of
reading Scripture out loud to hear what God might be saying to you through the
passage. Read Ecclesiastes 3:1-8. What stands out to you from these verses? Read
Ecclesiastes 3:1-8 again. What might God be telling you? Take time to write down
what you are hearing from God in these verses.

Come Together

Come Together

Supplies: Class Pack, Celebrate Wonder Bible Storybook, *Wonder Box, green cloth, battery-operated candle, picture of a seed-to-tree life cycle*

Prepare Ahead: Set up a Wonder Table (see p. 3) with a green cloth, battery-operated candle, and a Wonder Box (see p. 3). Display the Unit 3 Bible Verse Poster (Class Pack—pp. 9 & 16) and Faith Word Poster (Class Pack—p. 21). Place the picture of a seed-to-tree life cycle inside the Wonder Box.

- Point to the Unit 3 Faith Word Poster (Class Pack—p. 21), and invite the children to wonder about what the word *Scripture* means.

- Invite the kids to join you in a circle.

SAY: This month we will hear stories about people who wrote passages in the Bible. This week we will read some of the writings from the Book of Ecclesiastes.

WONDER: What does a wise person do?

- In this curriculum, we recommend reading stories from the *Celebrate Wonder Bible Storybook.* Allow an elementary-age child to read the story, "Everything Has a Season" (pp. 120–121) from the storybook.

PRAY: Dear God, help us hear your love through the writings in our Bibles. Amen.

Everything Has a Season – Preschool

Supplies: Reproducible Kids' Book, crayons

Prepare Ahead: Photocopy "Everything Has a Season" (Reproducible 11A) for each child.

- Invite the preschoolers to use crayons to color the picture.

SAY: The writer of the Book of Ecclesiastes in the Bible wrote a poem about how everything has a time, just like the seasons.

ASK: Which season is your favorite?

Favorite Season – Younger Elementary

Supplies: *Reproducible Kids' Book, crayons*

Prepare: *Photocopy "Favorite Season" (Reproducible 11B) for each child.*

• Hand out a copy of "Favorite Season" to each child.

SAY: The writer of the Book of Ecclesiastes in the Bible wrote a poem about how everything has a time, just like the seasons.

ASK: Which season is your favorite?

• Invite the kids to draw a picture of their favorite season.

• Encourage them to share their pictures with the group.

Season Science – Older Elementary

Supplies: *Reproducible Kids' Book*

Prepare Ahead: *Photocopy "Season Science" (Reproducible 11C) for each child.*

• Hand out a copy of "Season Science" to each child.

SAY: The writer of the Book of Ecclesiastes wrote a poem about how everything has a time, just like the seasons.

ASK: What do you know about the changing of the seasons?

SAY: Let's learn more about the science behind our changing seasons.

• Invite the kids to take turns reading the worksheet sections out loud.

Ecclesiastes Clock – All Ages

Supplies: *Reproducible Kids' Book, card stock, crayons or markers, scissors, hole punch, brads*

Prepare Ahead: *Photocopy "Ecclesiastes Clock" (Reproducible 11D) on card stock for each child.*

SAY: The writer of the bible book Ecclesiastes wrote a poem about how everything has a time. Make a special Ecclesiastes Clock to measure time like the writer.

• Hand out copies of Reproducible 11D.

• Invite the kids to color the circles on the worksheet.

• Help the kids cut out the two circles on their worksheets.

• Help the kids cut out the window on the top circle.

• Help the kids punch a hole in the center of both circles.

• Invite the kids to place the circle with the window over the second circle.

• Encourage the kids to attach the top circle to the bottom circle with a brad.

Wonder Time

Interactive Bible Story

Supplies: *Reproducible Kids' Book*

Prepare Ahead: *Photocopy "Everything Has a Season" (Reproducible 11F) for each child.*

• Invite several readers to take turns reading the story one section at a time.

WONDER: Where is God in this Scripture?

Share a Story

Supplies: *Celebrate Wonder DVD, TV, DVD player*

• Invite the children to join you and to sit in a circle on the floor.

• Watch the Session 11 video (Celebrate Wonder DVD).

Wonder with Me

Supplies: *Class Pack, Wonder Box, scissors*

Prepare Ahead: *Lay out the Wonder Story Mat for Unit 3 (Class Pack—pp. 7 & 18). Cut out the Bible story figures (Class Pack—p.3).*

• Place the Wonder Box on the Unit 3 Wonder Story Mat.

• Show the children the Unit 3 Faith Word Poster (Class Pack—p. 21).

SAY: Today's faith word is *Scripture*. *Scripture* is God's living word.

• Show the children this week's figure—a scroll with Ecclesiastes 3:1 on it.

WONDER together:

○ What is something happy that has happened this week?
How was God with you?

○ What is something sad that has happened this week?
How was God with you?

○ Sometimes we see God through nature or other people.
When have you seen God this week?

• Place the figure on the Wonder Story Mat.

• Open the Wonder Box to reveal the picture of a seed-to-tree life cycle.

WONDER: Why do you think a picture of a seed-to-tree life cycle is in the Wonder Box this week?

Experience Wonder

We Are Never Alone

Supplies: paper, markers or colored pencils

SAY: No matter what time it is in our lives, God is always with us. We can find God through our breath, through prayer, through friends or family, and through the stories in our Bible.

ASK: Which Bible story was your favorite?

SAY: We're going to illustrate our favorite Bible stories. I invite you to take these pictures home and hang them in your rooms to remind you that God is always with you.

- Invite the kids to draw a picture of their favorite Bible story.

- Encourage them to share their pictures with the group.

WONDER: How do you know God is with you?

Examine the Bible Verse

SAY: Our Unit 3 Bible verse is John 1:1. Find it in your Bibles.

ASK: Is John in the Old or New Testament? *(New)* Where is the Book of John located in the New Testament? *(fourth book)* In what chapter of John is our verse located? *(1)* What is the verse number? *(1)*

SAY: Our Bible has lots of wise things to teach us!

WONDER: What does this verse teach you?

- Gather the kids around the Bible Verse Poster (Class Pack—pp. 9 & 16). Read it together.

Peaceful Place

Supplies: Leader Guide—p. 115, Celebrate Wonder Bible Storybook, book: Four Seasons Make a Year, by Anne Rockwell; paper; crayons or markers

Prepare Ahead: Photocopy the Unit 3 Faith Word coloring sheet (Leader Guide—p. 115) for each child.

- Assist the children, as needed, as they interact with the items provided.

- Have each child color the Faith Word coloring sheet.

Tip: All of the supplies/activities suggested for the Peaceful Place are optional.

Go in Peace

Spiritual Practice – Exploring Scripture Through Writing.

Supplies: paper, pens or pencils

SAY: A spiritual practice is something we do to help us be present with God. A spiritual practice can be anything because you can be with God any time, anywhere, and any way! This month we are going to connect with God through writing.

- Guide the children through a spiritual practice:
  - ❍ **SAY:** Writing down our thoughts and feelings can connect us to God. Let's take a deep breath. Close your eyes. Take a deep breath. What do you feel? Take a deep breath. What do you think? Take a deep breath. Open your eyes.
  - ❍ Give each child a piece of paper and encourage them to write (or draw) what they feel and think today.
  - ❍ **WONDER:** Where is God when we feel and think these things?

SAY: God is always with us and isn't scared of any of our thoughts or feelings.

ASK: Would any of you like to share what you are thinking and feeling?

PRAY: Repeat after me: "God, we are so glad you are always with us. Amen."

- Bless the children before they leave. Touch each child on the hand as you say this blessing: "May you feel God's love all around you every day."

Family Spiritual Practice

Supplies: Reproducible Kids' Book; Leader Guide—pp. 111, 112

Prepare Ahead: Photocopy "Celebration Chart" (p. 111) and "Family Letter" (p. 112) for each child.

SAY: Let's take a look at your Take-Home Pages (*Reproducibles 11F–11G*). Ask your family to read the Bible story and participate in this week's spiritual devotion with you. There's an extra activity for you to do sometime this week.

- Send home a copy of the Take-Home Pages, a copy of the Family Letter, and a copy of the Celebration Chart with each child.

Supplemental Activities

Preschoolers – I Spy Growing!

SAY: Everything has a season and everything has a time to grow.

ASK: How do you know you are growing?

SAY: Yes! You know you're growing when you get taller, when you learn new things, and when you have to buy new shoes.

SAY: We're going to walk around the church and see if we can spy some other signs of growing!

- Invite the kids to walk around the church with you.

- Encourage them to point out anything they see that reminds them of growth.

Early Elementary – Seasons Charades

Supplies: Reproducible Kids' Book, basket or bowl

Prepare Ahead: Photocopy "Seasons Charades" (Reproducible 11E). Cut the cards out and place them in a basket or bowl.

SAY: We're going to take turns acting out the things on the cards. The rest of us will guess what you are doing and then guess which season we'd do that in.

- Choose one child to draw a card. Encourage them to act out what the card says.

- The rest of the group will guess what the child is doing and what season we would do that in.

- Choose another child to act out a card and have the group guess.

- Continue playing until all of the cards have been acted out.

Older Elementary – God's Eye

Supplies: craft sticks, yarn

SAY: The writer of Ecclesiastes 3:1-8 wanted to make sure everyone knew that no matter what was going on in their lives, God was with them. We're going to make God's eyes to remind us that God is always with us.

- Give each child two craft sticks and some yarn.
- Invite the kids to make a cross with the sticks. Tie the sticks together using yarn. Tie a knot around the sticks and then wrap the yarn several times until the sticks feel sturdy in the cross shape.
- Begin weaving the yarn around the sticks. Loop the yarn around one of the sticks. Take the yarn to the next stick, loop it, and pull the yarn to the next stick.
- Keep looping around the sticks until you have a square formed in the middle of the cross. Tie a knot with the yarn.

Intergenerational Activity – Seasonal Painting

Supplies: watercolor paints, card stock, paintbrushes, cups of water

SAY: No matter what time it is in our lives, God is always with us. We can find God through our breath, through prayer, through friends or family, and through the stories in our Bible. We can also find God in nature.

ASK: What's your favorite spot in nature?

ASK: What's your favorite season?

SAY: We're going to paint a picture of our favorite spot in nature in our favorite season.

- Invite each participant to paint a picture on a piece of card stock using the watercolor paints.
- Encourage the participants to share their pictures with the group.

PRAY: Dear God, thank you for always being with us. Help us notice you this week everywhere we go. Amen.

In the beginning was the Word and the Word was with God and the Word was God. (John 1:1)

Paul Writes to the Corinthians – 1 Corinthians 12:12-31

Prepare to Wonder

Faith Word: SCRIPTURE

Today's Bible story is from the letter Paul wrote to the church at Corinth. He heard that the Christians in Corinth were struggling and arguing among themselves over who was most important. Paul wrote to his friends at Corinth to remind them that each person is important in their own way. To help make his point, Paul uses a metaphor of the human body.

Paul uses the metaphor in two ways. First, Paul addresses those members of the Corinthian church who have low self-esteem and wish they were other than they are. Secondly, Paul uses the metaphor to address those who are suffering from an inflated sense of importance and look down on others.

The message to those suffering from low self-esteem and those with an inflated sense of importance is the same. Just as every part of the body is important and has its own purpose, every person is important and has a job to do. If one part of the body were missing, the body would not be the same. If even one person is missing from the church, the church is not the same. Everyone is given a spiritual gift and God uses all of our gifts for the common good.

Spiritual Practice for Adults

This month, we will try out the spiritual practice called *lectio divina*. It's a practice of reading Scripture out loud to hear what God might be saying to you through the passage. Read 1 Corinthians 12:12-31. What stands out to you from these verses? Read 1 Corinthians 12:12-31 again. What might God be telling you? Take time to write down what you are hearing from God in these verses.

Come Together

Come Together

Supplies: Class Pack, Celebrate Wonder Bible Storybook, Wonder Box, green cloth, battery-operated candle, age-appropriate picture of the anatomy of a human body

Prepare Ahead: Set up a Wonder Table (see p. 3) with a green cloth, battery-operated candle, and a Wonder Box (see p. 3). Display the Unit 3 Bible Verse Poster (Class Pack—pp. 9 & 16) and Faith Word Poster (Class Pack—p. 21). Place the picture of the anatomy of a human body inside the Wonder Box.

- Point to the Unit 3 Faith Word Poster (Class Pack—p. 21), and invite the children to wonder about what the word *Scripture* means.

- Invite the kids to join you in a circle.

SAY: This month we will hear stories about people who wrote passages in the Bible. This week we will read some of the writings Paul wrote in a letter to followers of Jesus in a town called Corinth.

- In this curriculum, we recommend reading stories from the *Celebrate Wonder Bible Storybook*. Allow an elementary-age child to read the story, "One Body" (pp. 302–303) from the storybook.

PRAY: Dear God, help us hear your love through the writings in our Bibles. Amen.

Paul Writes to the Corinthians – Preschool

Supplies: Reproducible Kids' Book, crayons

Prepare Ahead: Photocopy "Paul Writes to the Corinthians" (Reproducible 12A) for each child.

- Invite the preschoolers to use crayons to color the picture.

SAY: The New Testament has several letters Paul wrote to other believers. One of the letters is called 1st Corinthians. In this letter, Paul tells the believers in Corinth that everyone has a special gift to contribute to the faith community.

ASK: What is your special gift?

What's Different? – Younger Elementary

Supplies: Reproducible Kids' Book, crayons

Prepare: Photocopy "What's Different?" (Reproducible 12B) for each child.

• Hand out a copy of "What's Different?" to each child.

SAY: One of the letters Paul wrote is called 1st Corinthians. In this letter, Paul tells the believers in Corinth that everyone has a special gift to contribute to the faith community.

ASK: What is your special gift?

• Invite the kids to find and circle the differences between image 1 and 2, then color the picture.

Missing Vowels – Older Elementary

Supplies: Reproducible Kids' Book, pens or pencils

Prepare Ahead: Photocopy "Missing Vowels" (Reproducible 12C) for each child.

• Hand out a copy of "Missing Vowels" to each child.

SAY: This month we are learning about Scripture—God's living word. We are exploring Scripture through writing.

ASK: What is your favorite Scripture?

• Invite the kids to solve the puzzle by replacing the missing vowels.

Spread the Good News – All Ages

Supplies: Reproducible Kids' Book, crayons or markers

Prepare Ahead: Photocopy "Spread the Good News" (Reproducible 12D) for each child.

SAY: The New Testament has several letters Paul wrote to other believers. One of the letters is called 1st Corinthians. In this letter, Paul tells the believers in Corinth that everyone has a special gift to contribute to the faith community.

• Hand out copies of Reproducible 12D.

SAY: Think about what gifts you think God has given you and write them down inside the person outline. Then think about how you can use those gifts to do God's work and write those ideas at the bottom of the page.

• Invite the kids to draw or write their special qualities and talents inside the human outline.

• Encourage the kids to draw or write how they can use those gifts around the human outline.

• Encourage the kids to share their pictures with the group.

Wonder Time

Interactive Bible Story

Supplies: Reproducible Kids' Book

Prepare Ahead: Photocopy "One Body" (Reproducible 12F) for each child.

- Invite several readers to take turns reading the story one section at a time.

WONDER: Where is God in this Scripture?

Share a Story

Supplies: Celebrate Wonder DVD, TV, DVD player

- Invite the children to join you and to sit in a circle on the floor.
- Watch the Session 12 video (Celebrate Wonder DVD).

Wonder with Me

Supplies: Class Pack, Wonder Box, scissors

Prepare Ahead: Lay out the Wonder Story Mat for Unit 3 (Class Pack—pp. 7 & 18). Cut out the Bible story figures (Class Pack—p.3).

- Place the Wonder Box on the Unit 3 Wonder Story Mat.
- Show the children the Unit 3 Faith Word Poster (Class Pack—p. 21).

SAY: Today's faith word is *Scripture*. Scripture is God's living word.

- Show the children this week's figure—a scroll with 1 Corinthians 12:12 on it.

WONDER together:

   ❍ How do you think the people in the story felt?

   ❍ Share a time when you worked in a group and it went well.

   ❍ Where have you seen God this week?

- Place the figure on the Wonder Story Mat.
- Open the Wonder Box to reveal the picture of the anatomy of a human body.

WONDER: Why do you think a picture of the anatomy of a human body is in the Wonder Box this week?

Experience Wonder

Collaborative Painting

Supplies: butcher paper, tempura paint, paintbrushes, cups of water, paper plates, smocks

Prepare Ahead: Cut butcher paper into a 6-foot piece. Pour paints onto paper plates making a paint palate for each child. Give each child a painting smock.

SAY: Paul reminded the followers of Jesus that we should work together.

ASK: What is your favorite part of working together?

SAY: We're going to work together to make a beautiful painting!

- Invite the kids to use the paints to create an abstract work of art.

- Encourage them to collaborate and cooperate with one another.

WONDER: Why do you think it is important to God for us to work together?

Examine the Bible Verse

SAY: Our Unit 3 Bible verse is John 1:1. Find it in your Bibles.

ASK: Is John in the Old or New Testament? *(New)* Where is the Book of John located in the New Testament? *(fourth book)* In what chapter of John is our verse located? *(1)* What is the verse number? *(1)*

SAY: Our Bible has lots of wise things to teach us!

WONDER: What does this verse teach you?

- Gather the kids around the Bible Verse Poster (Class Pack—pp. 9 & 16). Read it together.

Peaceful Place

Supplies: Leader Guide—p. 115, Celebrate Wonder Bible Storybook, *book:* Bird Hugs, *by Ged Adamsonl; paper; crayons or markers*

Prepare Ahead: Photocopy the Unit 3 Faith Word coloring sheet (Leader Guide—p. 115) for each child.

- Assist the children, as needed, as they interact with the items provided.

- Have each child color the Faith Word coloring sheet.

Tip: All of the supplies/activities suggested for the Peaceful Place are optional.

Go in Peace

Spiritual Practice – Exploring Scripture Through Writing

Supplies: paper, pens or pencils

SAY: A spiritual practice is something we do to help us be present with God. A spiritual practice can be anything because you can be with God any time, anywhere, and any way! This month we are going to connect with God through writing.

- Guide the children through a spiritual practice:

  - ❍ **SAY:** Writing down our thoughts and feelings can connect us to God. Let's take a deep breath. Close your eyes. Take a deep breath. What do you feel? Take a deep breath. What do you think? Take a deep breath. Open your eyes.

  - ❍ Give each child a piece of paper and encourage them to write (or draw) what they feel and think today.

  - ❍ **WONDER:** Where is God when we feel and think these things?

SAY: God is always with us and isn't scared of any of our thoughts or feelings.

ASK: Would any of you like to share what you are thinking and feeling?

PRAY: Repeat after me: "God, we are so glad you are always with us. Amen."

- Bless the children before they leave. Touch each child on the hand as you say this blessing: "May you feel God's love all around you every day."

Family Spiritual Practice

Supplies: Reproducible Kids' Book; Leader Guide—pp. 111, 112

Prepare Ahead: Photocopy "Celebration Chart" (p. 111) and "Family Letter" (p. 112) for each child.

SAY: Let's take a look at your Take-Home Pages (Reproducibles 12F–12G). Ask your family to read the Bible story and participate in this week's spiritual devotion with you. There's an extra activity for you to do sometime this week.

- Send home a copy of the Take-Home Pages, a copy of the Family Letter, and a copy of the Celebration Chart with each child.

Supplemental Activities

Preschoolers – Body Connect

SAY: Today we've been talking about parts of the body. I'm going to give you some pairs of body parts. Each time I name a pair, move your body so that those two body parts are touching.

- Read the following pairs and encourage the children to move:
  - ○ hand-eye
  - ○ elbow-knee
  - ○ ear-shoulder
  - ○ finger-toe
  - ○ foot-knee
  - ○ hand-shoulder

SAY: Paul reminded us that we each make up the body of Christ. "The Body of Christ" is a fancy way of saying the church. We all make the church!

SING: I am the church! You are the church!
We are the church together!
All who follow Jesus,
all around the world!
Yes, we're the church together!

Early Elementary – Separate Parts

Supplies: paper, markers, tape

Prepare Ahead: Write each of the following words on a separate piece of paper: eyes, ears, mouth, hands, feet. Tape each paper up in a different part of the room.

- Divide the children into five groups.
- Have each group of children stand by a different sign.

SAY: For this activity, you are the body part on the sign posted near you.

ASK: Where are the eyes? (Expect the eyes group to answer.)

SAY: How are you answering me? You can't speak.

ASK: Where are the mouths? (Expect the mouths to answer.)

SAY: How did you hear my question? You are not ears.

ASK: Is there any group that could hear my command and respond? (Not unless the command was to wriggle your ears. Then the ears could respond.)

SAY: There isn't much that the body parts can do separately. Let's try working together. Give all the children permission to use all of their body parts to listen and respond to your question.

SAY: Suppose that I ask you to bring me a book.

ASK: What part would each group play?

• Encourage each group to tell what it would do to complete the task.

SAY: Each body part has a role to play and they are all important.

Older Elementary – Mind Map Doodle Prayer

Supplies: Reproducible Kids' Book, markers

Prepare Ahead: Photocopy "Mind Map Doodle Prayer" (Reproducible 12E) for each child.

• Give each child a copy of "Mind Map Doodle Prayer" and some markers.

SAY: Each person is a part of the Body of Christ; that means YOU are a part of the Body of Christ.

ASK: What does this make you think of?

SAY: Use the mind map to help you pray about what it means to you to be a part of the Body of Christ.

• Invite the kids to fill out the mind map with their ideas.

Intergenerational Activity – Body Collage

Supplies: magazines, scissors, glue, paper

Prepare Ahead: Go through the magazines and remove pages containing inappropriate content or images.

• Give each participant a piece of paper.

• Show the participants the magazines.

SAY: Today I want you to make a picture of a person. Your challenge is to use a different picture for each part of your person. Look through the magazines for pictures of people and then combine different parts from each picture to make your person.

• Have each participant cut out pictures from the magazines and glue them onto their paper to make a person.

In the beginning was the Word and the Word was with God and the Word was God. (John 1:1)

Paul Writes to the Philippians – Philippians 4:8-9, 13

Prepare to Wonder

Faith Word: SCRIPTURE

Today's Bible story is from the letter Paul wrote to the church at Philippi. He was in prison for preaching about Jesus when he wrote the letter to the Philippians. Paul heard the Philippians were having major conflict and Paul wanted to encourage the followers to follow the example of Jesus.

The encouragement Paul gives to the Philippians is rooted in positive thought. Paul knew that what we think, what we focus on, affects what we notice and what we see. What we think and believe, then affects what we do. If we focus on "all that is true, all that is holy, all that is just, all that is pure, all that is lovely, and all that is worthy of praise" (v.8), we will live like Jesus.

Spiritual Practice for Adults

This month, we will try out the spiritual practice called *lectio divina*. It's a practice of reading Scripture out loud to hear what God might be saying to you through the passage. Read Philippians 4:8-9, 13. What stands out to you from these verses? Read Philippians 4:8-9, 13 again. What might God be telling you? Take time to write down what you are hearing from God in these verses.

Come Together

Come Together

Supplies: Class Pack, Celebrate Wonder Bible Storybook, *Wonder Box, green cloth, battery-operated candle, Bible*

Prepare Ahead: Set up a Wonder Table (see p. 3) with a green cloth, battery-operated candle, and a Wonder Box (see p. 3). Display the Unit 3 Bible Verse Poster (Class Pack—pp. 9 & 16) and Faith Word Poster (Class Pack—p. 21). Place the Bible inside the Wonder Box.

- Point to the Unit 3 Faith Word Poster (Class Pack—p. 21), and invite the children to wonder about what the word *Scripture* means.
- Invite the kids to join you in a circle.

SAY: This month we will hear stories about people who wrote passages in the Bible. This week we will read some of the writings Paul wrote in a letter to followers of Jesus in a town called Philippi.

- In this curriculum, we recommend reading stories from the *Celebrate Wonder Bible Storybook.* Allow an elementary-age child to read the story, "Paul Writes the Philippians" (pp. 308–309) from the storybook.

PRAY: Dear God, help us hear your love through the writings in our Bibles. Amen.

Paul Writes to the Philippians – Preschool

Supplies: Reproducible Kids' Book, crayons

Prepare Ahead: Photocopy "Paul Writes to the Philippians" (Reproducible 13A) for each child.

- Invite the preschoolers to use crayons to color the picture.

SAY: The New Testament has several letters Paul wrote to other believers. One of the letters is called Philippians. Paul encourages the believers in Philippi to live like Jesus.

WONDER: How can you live like Jesus?

Bible Bookmarks – Younger Elementary

Supplies: Reproducible Kids' Book, crayons, scissors, card stock

Prepare: Photocopy "Bible Bookmarks" (Reproducible 13B) for each child on card stock.

- Hand out a copy of "Bible Bookmarks" to each child.

SAY: The stories in the Bible can be encouraging! Make a few bookmarks to use in your Bible to mark the stories that encourage you the most.

- Invite the kids to color the bookmarks.

- Help the kids cut out the bookmarks.

- Remind the kids to use their bookmarks at home.

Unit 3 Word Search – Older Elementary

Supplies: *Reproducible Kids' Book, pens or pencils*

Prepare Ahead: *Photocopy "Unit 3 Word Search" (Reproducible 13C) for each child.*

- Hand out a copy of "Unit 3 Word Search" to each child.

SAY: We learned a lot about Scripture this month!

ASK: What do you remember?

- Invite the kids to solve the puzzle and circle the words in the word bank.

August Stars and Constellations – All Ages

Supplies: *Reproducible Kids' Book*

Prepare Ahead: *Photocopy "August Stars and Constellations" (Reproducible 13D) for each child.*

- Hand out copies of Reproducible 9D.

- Invite the kids to look over the stars, constellations, and star pictures on the page.

ASK: Do you recognize any of the star pictures on the page?

- Invite the kids to share any star pictures they recognize. This sheet shows the same stars and constellations that we saw in May. Use this opportunity to see if any kids in your class have tried to find star pictures in the sky.

SAY: This fall, we began looking at the night sky to see star pictures. If you are having trouble finding these shapes, here's a tip.

- Point to Orion on the star chart.

SAY: Orion is the figure of a man. His belt has three bright stars that are pretty easy to find in the winter sky. If you can find the belt, you might be able to find some of the other stars and constellations on the sheet. This is the last time I will send home a star chart.

- Invite the kids to take the sheets home and look at the sky.

Wonder Time

Interactive Bible Story

Supplies: Reproducible Kids' Book

Prepare Ahead: Photocopy "Paul Writes to the Philippians" (Reproducible 13F) for each child.

- Invite several readers to take turns reading the story one section at a time.

WONDER: Where is God in this Scripture?

Share a Story

Supplies: Celebrate Wonder DVD, TV, DVD player

- Invite the children to join you and to sit in a circle on the floor.
- Watch the Session 13 video (Celebrate Wonder DVD).

Wonder with Me

Supplies: Class Pack, Wonder Box, scissors

Prepare Ahead: Lay out the Wonder Story Mat for Unit 3 (Class Pack—pp. 7 & 18). Cut out the Bible story figures (Class Pack—p.3).

- Place the Wonder Box on the Unit 3 Wonder Story Mat.
- Show the children the Unit 3 Faith Word Poster (Class Pack—p. 21).

SAY: Today's faith word is *Scripture*. Scripture is God's living word.

- Show the children this week's figure—a scroll with Philippians 4:9 on it.

WONDER together:

- ○ What does encouragement feel like?
- ○ What good things do you like to think about?
- ○ Where have you seen God this week?

- Place the figure on the Wonder Story Mat.
- Open the Wonder Box to reveal the Bible.

WONDER: Why do you think a Bible is in the Wonder Box this week?

Experience Wonder

Books of the New Testament Memory

Supplies: Reproducible Kids' Book, scissors

Prepare Ahead: Make two copies of the "Books of the New Testament" (Reproducible 13E). Cut the cards apart.

SAY: There are 27 books in the New Testament. Paul wrote several of the books in the New Testament. This month we read from two—1 Corinthians and Philippians.

- Place the cards facedown.
- Invite the kids to take turns playing memory with the cards.

WONDER: What is your favorite book of the Bible?

Tip: To play this game with preschoolers, add images or stickers to the names of the books of the Bible to help them find the matches.

Examine the Bible Verse

SAY: Our Unit 3 Bible verse is John 1:1. Find it in your Bibles.

ASK: Is John in the Old or New Testament? *(New)* Where is the Book of John located in the New Testament? *(fourth book)* In what chapter of John is our verse located? *(1)* What is the verse number? *(1)*

SAY: Our Bible has lots of wise things to teach us!

WONDER: What does this verse teach you?

- Gather the kids around the Bible Verse Poster (Class Pack—pp. 9 & 16). Read it together.

Peaceful Place

Supplies: Leader Guide—p. 115, Celebrate Wonder Bible Storybook, book: Horton Hears a Who, by Dr. Seuss; paper; crayons or markers

Prepare Ahead: Photocopy the Unit 3 Faith Word coloring sheet (Leader Guide—p. 115) for each child.

- Assist the children, as needed, as they interact with the items provided.
- Have each child color the Faith Word coloring sheet.

Tip: All of the supplies/activities suggested for the Peaceful Place are optional.

Go in Peace

Spiritual Practice – Exploring Scripture Through Writing

Supplies: paper, pens or pencils

SAY: A spiritual practice is something we do to help us be present with God. A spiritual practice can be anything because you can be with God any time, anywhere, and any way! This month we are going to connect with God through writing.

- Guide the children through a spiritual practice:
  - ○ **SAY:** Writing down our thoughts and feelings can connect us to God. Let's take a deep breath. Close your eyes. Take a deep breath. What do you feel? Take a deep breath. What do you think? Take a deep breath. Open your eyes.
  - ○ Give each child a piece of paper and encourage them to write (or draw) what they feel and think today.
  - ○ **WONDER:** Where is God when we feel and think these things?

SAY: God is always with us and isn't scared of any of our thoughts or feelings.

ASK: Would any of you like to share what you are thinking and feeling?

PRAY: Repeat after me: "God, we are so glad you are always with us. Amen."

- Bless the children before they leave. Touch each child on the hand as you say this blessing: "May you feel God's love all around you every day."

Family Spiritual Practice

Supplies: Reproducible Kids' Book; Leader Guide—pp. 111, 112

Prepare Ahead: Photocopy "Celebration Chart" (p. 111) and "Family Letter" (p. 112) for each child.

SAY: Let's take a look at your Take-Home Pages (*Reproducibles 13F–13G*). Ask your family to read the Bible story and participate in this week's spiritual devotion with you. There's an extra activity for you to do sometime this week.

- Send home a copy of the Take-Home Pages, a copy of the Family Letter, and a copy of the Celebration Chart with each child.

Supplemental Activities

Preschoolers – Sandbox Writing

Supplies: *sand tray, sand*

Prepare Ahead: *Put the sand into the sand tray.*

SAY: This month we have been learning the word *Scripture.* We're going to practice writing the word in sand.

- Invite the kids to practice writing the word *Scripture* in the sand.
- After everyone has gotten to try writing *Scripture*, allow the kids to play in the sand.

Early Elementary – Don't Let the Balloon Touch the Ground

Supplies: *balloon*

Prepare Ahead: *Blow up the balloon.*

- Toss the balloon up in the air.
- Encourage the kids to keep the balloon off the ground.
- Play a few rounds.

SAY: Paul wanted to encourage, or lift up, the followers in Philippi.

WONDER: Who has encouraged you?

Older Elementary – Friendship Bracelets

Supplies: embroidery thread, scissors

- Allow each kid to choose three colors of string. Cut each string three feet long.

- Invite the kids to tie their three strings together with a knot at the top.

- Help each child braid their strings together.

- Encourage the kids to give their bracelets to a friend.

SAY: Showing kindness is a way of sharing encouragement.

ASK: Who will you share your bracelet with?

Intergenerational Activity – Illustrate Your Favorite Bible Story

Supplies: paper, markers or crayons

- Give each participant a piece of paper.

SAY: We've heard a lot of Bible stories this year.

ASK: Which story was your favorite?

WONDER: Why do you think that story stands out to you?

- Encourage the participants to illustrate their favorite story.

- Invite the participants to share their pictures with the group.

CELEBRATE WONDER® Celebration Chart

Place this chart on your refrigerator, kitchen table, or in an easy-to-access place. Throughout the week, have your child mark a space each time he or she completes an item on the chart. When a vertical, horizontal, or diagonal line is completed, celebrate together!

CELEBRATE

I made peace after a fight.	I tried to see someone else's view.	I showed peace.	I prayed for peace.	I was kind to a family member.
I wondered about something.	I noticed awe in nature.	I asked a hard question.	I saw God working in the world.	I learned something new.
I trusted God.	I was trustworthy today.	Free Celebration!	I shared something important with a friend or family member.	I trusted in God's love.
I prayed.	I spent time with my Bible.	I wondered about a Bible story.	I talked about a Bible story.	I learned a new Bible story.
I played with a new friend.	I went outside.	I cooked something.	I saw God in a friend.	I helped someone in my family.

PARENT GUILT: The Problem With Perfection

I participated in a wonderful youth group when I was in high school. My youth leader talked about the importance of praying every day, reading Scripture, and living a moral life. I began setting my alarm 20 minutes early so that I could start my day off right. I'd pray and read the Bible. Unfortunately, this time quickly turned into the newest way I wasn't good enough. I would oversleep 10 minutes and beat myself up all through the remaining 10 minutes. I resented these practices and I resented myself for not being a better person.

I have battled the pervasiveness of perfectionism for a long time. Our culture constantly pushes us to be the best. It's hard to imagine that God isn't looking for us to be perfect when it seems like everything else implicitly teaches us that, in order to be worthy people, we must be perfect people. One of the things I have to remind myself of when I get caught in the cycle of perfectionism is this: I don't have to do things perfectly to be a good, deserving person. In fact, striving to be perfect distracts from a true relationship with God and with God's people.

As a children's minister and mom, I have talked with several parents about this very thing showing up in our parenting. We feel guilty for all the ways we aren't "perfect" at helping our kids be good people of faith. Have you fallen prey to this perfectionism? Take a breath and remember the following things:

1. There is no one right way to be a teacher of faith for your child. Free yourself from the example you have in your mind about how raising your child to be a disciple of Christ should look. The first image of God a child has is based on your care of him or her. Hold, listen, play, read, and be present with your child. This act of being together creates a strong, loving, God-filled experience for you both.

2. There is not a specific amount of time you are required to "do faith." Susanna Wesley, the mother of John and Charles Wesley (the founders of the Methodist movement), believed that God was present in everything. She washed dishes and was with God. She cooked food and was with God. Instead of worrying about setting aside a special time, be attentive to the love that surrounds your family all the time. Use your time at the kitchen table, in the car, at bath time, and at bedtime for prayers and stories and fellowship.

3. You can say you don't know. There are no right answers to the many questions and wonderings faith brings. I encourage your family to embrace the mystery of God. Saying, "I don't know; let's learn about it together" is one of the greatest gifts you can give your child. It encourages imagination and opens your child to discovering how God is moving in the world.

Faith Word—Unit 1

Everything you need to lead faith formation with all ages in one classroom is found in this Kit.

Each week start by reviewing the session. Read the "Prepare to Wonder" section and do the spiritual practice for adults. This background information helps you navigate any questions your class may have. The spiritual practice helps prepare your heart for the coming class time.

When your class gathers, start by inviting the children into the classroom to mark their attendance on the Attendance Chart (Class Pack). Tell the children what Faith Word they will learn about that week. Let the children choose to do something from the Peaceful Place while you wait to start.

When you are ready to begin, invite all the children to join you to read the story from the *Celebrate Wonder Bible Storybook*. Then guide the preschoolers to do the coloring page, the younger-elementary kids to do their reproducible, and the older-elementary kids to do their reproducible. There is also always one activity everyone can do together. You may choose to do this instead of or in addition to the reproducible activities.

Next, your whole class will participate in an interactive retelling of the Bible story, watch the session's video from the *Celebrate Wonder DVD*, and wonder together. You will use the Wonder Story Mat (Class Pack), Faith Word Poster (Class Pack), and Wonder Box (see p. 3) during this time.

Then your class will respond to the story. There are activities to choose from: an all-ages activity, the Peaceful Place, and supplemental activities.

Finally, you will gather the group back together to participate in a spiritual practice and a blessing. You will send home the Take-Home Reproducible pages that include a retelling of the week's Bible story, a spiritual practice for the family to do together that week, and a pen-and-paper activity that each child can do on her or his own that week.

We have also included supplemental activities—one for preschoolers, one for early-elementary kids, one for older-elementary kids, and one for intergenerational groups. If your group leans more heavily with one of these ages, you are welcome to include one of these activities in your session.

You know your kids best. You know your volunteers best.

Some groups prefer to have more time to work alone, and some prefer to have more time to work together.

Some volunteers want to be able to choose their own activities, and some want you to have worked all of that out before they enter the room to lead the session. The most important part of ministry is connecting with one another as you grow together in God's love.

CELEBRATE WONDER
Using This Kit in an Age-Graded Ministry

Everything you need to lead faith formation with each age group in their own space is found in this Kit.

Each week start by reviewing the session. Read the "Prepare to Wonder" section and do the spiritual practice for adults. This background information helps you navigate any questions your class may have. The spiritual practice helps prepare your heart for the coming class time. Include this page in the packet you prepare for each volunteer.

Preschool Groups

Start by inviting the children into their classrooms to mark their attendance on the Attendance Chart (Class Pack). Tell the children what Faith Word they will learn that week. Let the children choose to do something from the Peaceful Place while you wait to start.

When you are ready to begin, invite all of the children to join you to read the story from the *Celebrate Wonder Bible Storybook*. Then guide the preschoolers to do the coloring page. Next, your class will listen to an interactive retelling of the Bible story, watch the session's video from the *Celebrate Wonder DVD*, and wonder together. You will use the Wonder Story Mat (Class Pack), Faith Word Poster (Class Pack), and Wonder Box (see p. 3) during this time.

Then your class will respond to the story. There are activities to choose from: an any-ages activity, the Peaceful Place, and the supplemental activity for preschoolers. Choose one activity for everyone to do together, and then allow the children to play in the Peaceful Place.

Early Elementary Groups

Start by inviting the children into their classrooms to mark their attendance on the Attendance Chart (Class Pack). Tell the children what Faith Word they will learn that week. Let the children choose to do something from the Peaceful Place while you wait to start.

When you are ready to begin, invite all of the children to join you to read the story from the *Celebrate Wonder Bible Storybook*. Then invite the children to do the early-elementary reproducible page. There is also always one Come Together activity that you can choose to include. You may choose to do this instead of or in addition to the reproducible page.

Next, your class will read an interactive retelling of the Bible story, watch the session's video from the *Celebrate Wonder DVD,* and wonder together. You will use the Wonder Story Mat (Class Pack), Faith Word Poster (Class Pack), and Wonder Box (see p. 3) during this time.

Then your class will respond to the story. There are activities to choose from: an any-ages activity, the Peaceful Place, and the early-elementary supplemental activity. Choose one activity for everyone to do together and then allow the children to play in the Peaceful Place.

Older Elementary Groups

Start by inviting the children into their classrooms to mark their attendance on the Attendance Chart (Class Pack). Tell the children what Faith Word they will learn that week. Let the children choose to do something from the Peaceful Place while you wait to start.

When you are ready to begin, invite the children to do the older-elementary reproducible page. Do the all-ages Come Together activity in addition to the reproducible page.

Next, your class will perform the interactive retelling of the Bible story, watch the session's video from the *Celebrate Wonder DVD,* and wonder together. You will use the Wonder Story Mat (Class Pack), Faith Word Poster (Class Pack), and Wonder Box (see p. 3) during this time.

Then your class will respond to the story. There are activities to choose from: an any-ages activity, the Peaceful Place, and the older-elementary supplemental activity. Choose one activity for everyone to do together and then allow the children to play in the Peaceful Place.

Everyone will end their time together this way:

Finally, you will gather the group back together to participate in a spiritual practice and a blessing. You will send home the Take-Home Reproducible pages that have a retelling of the week's Bible story, something for the family to do together that week, and a pen-and-paper activity that each child can do on his or her own that week.

Start with the Large Group Time:

1. Everyone will watch the session's video from the DVD.

2. Wonder together using the unit's Wonder Story Mat and Faith Word Poster found in the Class Pack. Show the class what is in the Wonder Box and ask them what that might have to do with this week's story.

3. Send the kids to their small groups.

Small Group Time:

1. Invite the children into their classrooms to mark their attendance on the Attendance Chart (Class Pack).

2. Read the Bible story from the *Celebrate Wonder Bible Storybook* or the Bible.

3. Do the reproducible that coordinates with the age group of your small group.

4. Do the any-ages activity, the interactive retelling of the Bible story, and then allow the children to play in the Peaceful Place.

5. Gather the group back together to participate in a spiritual practice and a blessing. You will send home the Take-Home Reproducible pages that include a retelling of the week's Bible story, something for the family to do together that week, and a pen-and-paper activity that each child can do on her or his own that week.

If your Small Group needs more:

We have also included supplemental activities—one for preschoolers, one for early-elementary kids, and one for older-elementary kids. If your group leans more heavily with one of these ages, you are welcome to include one of these activities in your session.

The Leader Guide will have to be moved around to create an easy-to-follow plan for your volunteer teachers. The easiest way to do this is to:

1. Open the PDF of the Leader Guide.

1a. If you have Adobe Acrobat Pro, go to File>Save As>Microsoft Word>Word Document. This will turn the PDF into a Word file.

1b. If you don't have Adobe Acrobat Pro, open Microsoft Word. You will select the text from the PDF and then paste it into the Word file.

2. Arrange the activities from each session in the order that makes the most sense for your kids and volunteers.

3. Print your version of the plan and place it in each classroom.

4. Email your version of the plan to your volunteers.

CELEBRATE WONDER® Using This Kit in Intergenerational Ministry

Everything you need to lead faith formation with all ages, including youth and adults, in one classroom is found in this Kit.

Each week start by reviewing the session. Read the "Prepare to Wonder" section and do the spiritual practice for adults. This background information helps you navigate any questions your class may have. The spiritual practice helps prepare your heart for the coming class time.

When your class gathers, start by inviting everyone into the classroom to mark their attendance on the Attendance Chart (Class Pack). Tell each participant what Faith Word they will learn about that week. Let everyone choose to do something from the Peaceful Place while you wait to start.

When you are ready to begin, invite everyone to join you to read the story from the *Celebrate Wonder Bible Storybook*. Then guide everyone to choose one of the reproducible activities to complete. There is also always one activity that everyone can do together. You may choose to do this instead of or in addition to the reproducible activities.

Next, your whole class will participate in the interactive retelling of the Bible story, watch the session's video from the *Celebrate Wonder DVD*, and wonder together. You will use the Wonder Story Mat (Class Pack), Faith Word Poster (Class Pack), and Wonder Box (see p. 3) during this time.

Then your class will respond to the story. There are activities to choose from: an all-ages activity, an intergenerational activity found in the supplemental activities section, and the Peaceful Place. Your group should do the intergenerational activity, then they can do any of the other activities that work well for your group.

Finally, you will gather the group back together to participate in a spiritual practice and a blessing. You will send home the Take-Home Reproducible pages that include a retelling of the week's Bible story, something for each family to do together that week, and a pen-and-paper activity that everyone can do on his or her own that week.

Everything you need to lead faith formation with your family at home is found in this Kit.

Each week start by reviewing the session. Read the "Prepare to Wonder" section and do the spiritual practice for adults. This background information helps you navigate any questions your kids may have. The spiritual practice helps prepare your heart for the time you will spend with your family.

When you are ready to begin, invite everyone to listen as the story is read from the *Celebrate Wonder Bible Storybook*. Then guide everyone to choose one of the reproducible activities to complete.

Next, watch the session's video from the *Celebrate Wonder DVD* and wonder together. You will use the Wonder Story Mat (Class Pack), Faith Word Poster (Class Pack), and Wonder Box (see p. 3) during this time.

Then respond to the story. There are activities to choose from: an all-ages activity, any of the supplemental activities, and the Peaceful Place. Your family can do any or all of these.

Finally, you will participate in a spiritual practice and a blessing.

Everything you need to lead faith formation virtually is found in this Kit.

Each week start by reviewing the session. Read the "Prepare to Wonder" section and do the spiritual practice for adults. This background information helps you navigate any questions your kids may have. The spiritual practice helps prepare your heart for the time you will spend together.

You can:

- Email each family the reproducible pages for the week. Encourage them to print off the pages for each person in their home, or

- Mail each family the reproducible pages for the week.

Invite each family to join you through an online video conference platform, like Zoom. Make sure to email the link the morning of the online gathering to remind your families that you will be hosting a faith-formation event.

When you are ready to begin, invite everyone to listen as the story is read from the *Celebrate Wonder Bible Storybook*. Then guide everyone to choose one of the reproducible activities to complete. You can use this time while everyone is working on their reproducible pages to catch up on joys and concerns.

Next, watch the session's video from the *Celebrate Wonder Downloadable DVD* and wonder together. You will use the Wonder Story Mat, Faith Word Poster, and Wonder Box (see p. 3) during this time.

Then respond to the story by doing the suggested art activity in the Peaceful Place and watching a YouTube video of the suggested book being read.

Finally, you lead the families in a spiritual practice and a blessing.

Zoom fatigue is real, AND our families want to stay connected in safe ways. Keep this gathering under thirty minutes, and be sure to use the time to catch up. Everyone is going through collective trauma, and they need you to be present more than they need you to teach them Bible stories.

Set up a Google Classroom or a Bitmoji Classroom using the digital assets. Your families will go through the lesson as they are able each week, instead of committing to a virtual meeting time.

Check out what Erica Kozlowski at Central United Methodist is doing in her Bitmoji Sunday School Room:

https://docs.google.com/presentation/d/1dJldspSipOK3Esorwj8Gz_d4eit7WdfWkVwHVKewt-s/edit#slide=id.p

 **Classroom Management Tips**

- Look over and plan your session before you get to your class.

- Greet the children at the door and involve them immediately in the session.

- Give a five-minute warning when it's time to move to a new activity.

- Give your children leadership roles. Preschoolers can be line leaders to help the children move to the story area. Older children can read the Bible story out loud. Be sure to ask for volunteers. If a child doesn't want to read aloud, let the child pass.

- Check for allergies before serving snacks.

- Always overplan. It's better to run out of time than to run short on a lesson.

- Review the session plan for resources you might need to gather that aren't in the church supplies.

- Gain the kids' attention.

- Ask the kids to look at you. Wait until everyone is looking. It's better for teachers to say, "Point your eyes toward me," and wait for compliance instead of saying, "Stop talking, turn around, and look at me."

- Start with small consequences. When a rule is broken, assign the smallest consequence possible and see if that gets the job done.

- Using appropriate curriculum is a classroom-management strategy.

- Assigning age-appropriate work eliminates the risk of kids not being able to do the activities.

- Rehearse transitions. Most disruptions occur between activities.

- Anticipate problems and be creative in preventing or handling them.

- Turn a problematic situation into a positive learning event.

- Find things to appreciate. Start class by looking for things to delight in.

- Create an inclusive environment.

- Be clear up front about expectations and intentions.

- Use inclusive language.

- Ask for clarification if you're unclear about a kid's question.

- Treat all of your kids with respect and consideration.

- Develop an awareness of barriers to learning (cultural, social, experiential).

- Provide sufficient time and space for kids to gather their thoughts and contribute to discussions.

- Use hand signals and other nonverbal communication.

- Sometimes the behavior of a single child can become so disruptive that you can't teach the session. Get help! If certain children are repeatedly disruptive, add more adults to your group, or ask parents and caregivers for helpful ways to care for and engage their child.

 **Registration Page**

Child's Name _____

Parent Name(s) _____

Address _____

_____

Phone _____

Child's Birthday _____ Age _____

Child's Brothers and Sisters:

Name _____ Age _____

Name _____ Age _____

Name _____ Age _____

Grandparents or other adults your child sees often and is close to:

_____

_____

Allergies or situations the teacher should know about:

_____

_____

_____

_____

Parent will be at:

_____

_____

_____